Merie Vision Publishing, LLC
www.merievisionpublishing.com

Copyright © 2025 by Angela Mitchell

ISBN: 978-1-961213-48-7

Library of Congress Control Number on record

All rights reserved. No part of this book may be reproduced in any form either by electronic or mechanical means, including information storage and retrieval systems, without written permission from the publisher, except by a reviewer who may quote brief images in a review.

Book Design and Editing by Merie Vision Publishing

Cover Design by Che'Von

First Print Edition July 2025

2 3 4 5

THE LOVE OF MY FATHER

ANGELA C. MITCHELL

To Mom and Dad,

Thank you for planting the seeds inside of me that are necessary for growth. You poured into me the wisdom, strength, and faith I needed to walk through life with purpose. You made sure I understood the most important decision I would ever face. To accept Christ and all the love, protection, and promises that comes with Him, or to choose Satan and carry the pain, confusion, and destruction that follow.

There was no rule book for raising five children. You did the best you could with what you had. That best was more than enough. You gave your heart, your prayers, and your sacrifice.

You will forever be honored. I love you always.

~Ang

The Mitchell's

Table Of Contents

The Forward
I

Chapter One
MY FIRST LOVE
Page 1

Chapter Two
THE LOSING FIGHT
Page 8

Chapter Three
LIFE IS FOR THE LIVING
Page 18

Chapter Four
THE LAST DRAW
Page 22

Chapter Five
INNOCENCE LOST
Page 27

Chapter Six
FAREWELL
Page 39

Chapter Seven
THIS AIN'T LOVE
Page 48

Chapter Eight
THE CONCEPTION STORY
Page 54

Chapter Nine
NOT AGAIN!
Page 72

Chapter Ten
NEVER SAY NEVER
Page 93

Chapter Eleven
THE MOVE
Page 102

Chapter Twelve
MY BROTHERS
Page 113

Chapter Thirteen
THE EMANCIPATION OF GIGI
Page 121

Chapter Fourteen
THE ELDER & THE PASTOR
Page 131

Chapter Fifteen
ACCOUNTABILITY
Page 151

Chapter Sixteen
THE LOVE OF MY FATHER
Page 154

THE FOREWORD

Being the youngest of five children can be tough, especially growing up in Newark, New Jersey. Everyone knows that dealing with a lifestyle of dysfunction is very common in urban neighborhoods. Your worst enemies could sometimes be your family.

The story being told is Angela's recollection of events leading up to her many relationships with men. She experienced the lack of love from her very own father, which, in turn, distorted her perception of many men and, most importantly, God. This is a true story of Angela that follows her pursuit of obtaining *real love* at any and *all* costs.

The last man that Angela was expecting to run into was Jesus Christ. Perhaps her encounter with him changed the overall course of her entire life. Can Angela find meaning when she finds him? You will experience her confused, lust-driven, and dramatic lifestyle as she goes through phases of hopelessness, disappointment, and despair while connecting herself with many men. Angela has yet to realize that men *cannot* and *will not* save her. The love she yearns for is ultimately the love of her father. You will read how it all began. Get ready to be taken on an emotional roller coaster, as Angela attempts to lead you through real-time, raw emotions of her experiences of sins, challenges, and ultimately, forgiveness. There are so many layers to this book, and this is just the beginning.

CHAPTER ONE: MY FIRST LOVE

My earliest memory of my father was when I was around one or two years of age. My mother was getting us both ready for Sunday's church service, but she decided to leave me at home with my dad. She placed me on his lap while he was lying on the couch and made her exit. I recall feeling very sad and utterly confused. I looked down at his face and began to weep. Then, I attempted to escape and get down. He held me tighter and told me to "shut up all that noise!" Whether or not I stopped crying, I do not remember. However, I do remember him giving me a Wise Crunchy Cheese Doodle in order to make me stop crying.

I felt abandoned!

How dare my mother deceive me? How dare she leave me all alone with this man who is mean to me? I feared my father to the utmost. His stature, his demeanor, his voice – I feared them all.

As he lay there and I sat on – what appeared to be more of his stomach – we watched the television. My memory is so keen that I even know the shows we were watching. *Go figure!*

It was a Sunday morning, which explains why Frederick K. Price was on the screen. He was a pastor and preacher who preached faith-based messages. He preached the Gospel of Jesus Christ. His theme song always brought me joy. After that went off, all of my dad's westerns came on; shows such as Bonanza, The Big Valley, and Wyatt Earp. My father loved these shows so much that he called himself Wyatt Earp. Personally, I never understood the correlation.

By the time my mom came back home, I was calm and full of snacks. She walked into the living room, and I remember running to her, grabbing her legs, and crying once again. I looked back at my father, relieved to see my mother. I felt at peace. I felt like I could breathe again. At the same time, I remained upset with her for leaving me with him in the first place.

There were so many things I recalled during my childhood about my dad. This man could do no wrong in my eyes. He was the true man of the house, especially seeing as though I had three brothers who also lived there. What he said was Golden. What he expressed to us all was performed one way or another. Although he was very strict and often angry and mean to his children, I still had respect for him and dared not to cross him. I looked at him as if he were the most powerful man alive. He was my first love and the first man I knew in general. The first example of a male I found was in him.

When he came home from working overnight, he would come in with a loud announcement. It's like he wanted the entire house to know that the "King" had arrived. All five of us would greet him in the living room, jump on his arms, and swing. As he struggled to pull us all up, I would be left in awe. Witnessing just how powerful and strong this man was, actually brought me joy.

"Daddy, you are so strong! How can you lift us all up?"

Then, he would sit down and tell us to pull off his dirty work boots. It would take every ounce of energy inside of us to pull off his boots and thermal socks, but it brought me joy.

My dad worked for Conrail Trains, and he was a Break Man. I'm not sure of his entire job description, but I just know he worked outside, and he worked overnight. On this particular night, it must have been a Friday because he came home pissy drunk. When Dad got drunk, he was louder than he normally was, but surprisingly, he wasn't as mean.

However, on this particular night, I woke up out of my sleep with a really sour stomach. I felt the presence of my father, but he wasn't home yet. I called for him, but Mommy said he wasn't home.

"Yes, he is, Mommy, because I can feel him!" I replied

Then, I proceeded to ask for the garbage can because I was about to throw up. My sister, Rae, ran out of the bed we both shared and got the garbage can for me. Simultaneously, I made a loud burp, and I could feel vomit entering my mouth. Crazy thing, my burp smelt as if I was drinking alcohol. My sister was disgusted! However, she did not leave me, and held my hair up.

I burped again, and then I screamed out, "It's coming. It's coming. I can feel it!"

Before I could utter another word, a huge ball seemed to come out of my throat! The vomit remained in tack and it looked just like a tennis ball. It didn't even break up. The biggest part was that it smelled exactly like fermented alcohol. Not like a sour tummy, but exactly as if I had a hangover, which couldn't have been true because I was only 5 years old.

I felt my father.

Whatever daddy was doing started to affect his baby girl – not in a good way. Immediately after that happened, here comes dad just as loud and drunk as always. Oddly enough, out of nowhere, he started to throw up as well. It was a very long night, to say the least.

My dad stood at 6 feet 2 inches tall, strong, athletic build, and thick, full hair. He had a milk chocolate complexion and wore a full beard. In my opinion, he was very handsome.

He preached the Gospel of Jesus Christ before he went off to Vietnam because he was in the Army. During this time, he met my mother while doing missionary work. They married when she was 20 years old and he was 21 years old.

My dad was enlisted for 2 years before he came home. When he came back, he was no longer the same man as he was before he left. Mommy would say that he fought and yelled in his sleep. Dad also kept diaries explaining the horrors of Vietnam. Now, we know that he came back home with PTSD. Unfortunately, during this time, they didn't treat the veterans with much care, if any, when they came back home. So, my father returned to my mother as a traumatized and broken man, who had to get a job and support his family.

In the midst of this unaddressed and uncared for condition, came six children. The first child was lost because my father gave my mother an STD that caused the miscarriage. The second child, a son named Timothy, was born, but he didn't last the entire day. Trust me, they don't make mothers like mine anymore. To have to endure such heartache, loss, pain, and STILL serve your husband? The women of my generation would have cut his dick clean off! The disrespect of it all!

Daddy did a little bit more than fight the war and be a nurse. He brought home a whole lot of treats, too. Treats that weren't even sweet and lives he ruined on the account of his own sins. Oh yeah, and terrible consequences that happen when you turn away from the Lord. Your sins and actions affect everything you're connected to and the things that come from you.

I'm sure all of us in that house have a story to tell. My mother can tell you her experiences, but my sister, and my three brothers have their own set of trauma.

Then there is me.

The last of five children.

This is my story of forgiveness, judgment, and deliverance.

My story, from the eyes of "the baby of the family." I've always wondered what happened between me and the many men I have had in my life. Well, it all started somewhere. It started with finding out that my dad was only *HUMAN*.

All my life, I have been running around trying to avoid men *like* my father. On the contrary, I was not looking for my father in other men – let some therapists tell you, they disagree with me.

My dad had it all, so it seemed. A new, beautiful wife, good church, loving family, and close friends. *What more do you need to be happy? To be drafted?* That's *exactly* what happened. He was drafted into the Vietnam War. The absence away from my mother and the horrors he must have seen, pushed him over the edge. All I know is that, that same man who was kind and loving came back home traumatized, lonely, confused, and full of demons. Not the kind of demons you can put into a closet. The kind that if not cast out, continues to multiply. The kind of multiplication that continues throughout generations. I'm pretty sure those evil seeds were sown all throughout my mother's womb. Even with the two miscarriages, they continued to all of us. No wonder we were so dysfunctional.

Growing up was so confusing. I had two parents who I never saw argue - maybe once, and that's a hard *maybe*. However, he stayed down our throats. He was very harsh on my brothers, especially towards my oldest brother. Like, there were episodes when my brother would play outside and get dirty. When he would come back into the house, my father would whoop him. My dad would get so angry with us so much that, we as children, started to rank our beatings.

Another time I can remember vividly was when I was nine years old. We had just moved into this new apartment and my youngest brother and I began to play in the living room. I started to jump rope – don't ask me why I wasn't jumping outside. However, we didn't realize my father was in the basement. Out of nowhere, he came upstairs screaming at us. Immediately afterward, he took out his belt and started swinging it. My brother received a few licks and ran out. I was left with my shorts on, which exposed all of my thighs. I remember screaming until I fell out or until my dad got tired. He would also do this thing where he would talk and beat us at the same time.

"DIDN'T...*whap*...I TELL...*whop*...YOU TO...*pow*... STOP MAKING...*bam*... ALL THAT...*whap*... DAMN NOISE!!"

Then, he just went back downstairs like nothing ever happened and left me on the floor, terrified and crying. Here comes my brother, peeking in from behind the door and asking if I was ok.

"You ran and left me, Nat!" I screamed.

He swears he thought I was behind him. My other brothers came to see the condition of my body. All I remember them saying was that my youngest brother had nothing to show for having been beaten. They said he got a "cheeseburger." Whereas, my legs were swollen with the exact shape of the belt. I had whelps everywhere!

You see, the belt my father beat us with was his work belt. Those belts had big snaps on them and they were wide – not like the common thin belts we wear today. His belts were real cowhide leather, made to endure the harsh weather and normal wear and tear. My brothers actually had respect for me enduring my father's rage. They said I had the "Big Mac!" That was the top-of-the-line burger, seeing as though we loved to eat McDonalds.

I went outside to be with my friends, but I was limping because I was in so much pain. Little did anyone know, the real pain was in my heart. I couldn't believe my father actually beat me worse than ever before. He broke me – not my body – he broke my heart. I couldn't look at him for days after that.

My mother came home from work very upset with him. I remember her telling him that he cannot beat me that hard and to not hit me out of anger. Of course, my father would never apologize to me. That was a joke!

Now, I knew I feared him more than before. Whenever he called me to do anything, I would jump no matter what it was. Big or small. My dad would literally call me from down the street to come inside to prepare a cup of ice for him. He would also call me inside to get the remote control, which would literally be one arm's reach from him.

On top of his cruel treatment, he would just appear to be angry for no reason that I understood.

Talk about displaced aggression!

He was hostile and appeared to gain power from the fear he invoked in his children. He never talked to me; he talked at me. Everything was rules and punishment with him. That was the only way he talked. He never asked me about my day or even if I needed anything. Honestly, I cannot recall my dad ever telling me that he loved me. According to my brothers, they never heard those words either.

Remember, everything I tell you is from the thoughts of a child; these are not my adult views. Although I am clear on my feelings then, even up until the actions, as a mother now, I understand discipline. I also understand abuse. We as children suffered emotional, spiritual, and physical abuse. The confusion between the two that existed in my home was surreal.

At times, we would go with my father to church and watch him preach. Before we walked back into the house, he was yelling and threatening us. On his days off from work, we saw him drunk, but then he was actually having fun. My brothers enjoyed imitating him, but I didn't like that at all. He was just a little too friendly for my liking when he was drunk. Just as he did with my sister, he would have me sit on his lap. He liked when I played with his beard and gave him kisses, but then he made me get off of him. Unfortunately, with my older sister, when she was a teenager, my father had her sit on his lap in a manner that no father should ever do with their children. Whatever it was that happened, he did not allow it to go there with me.

Eventually, we got to a point where I couldn't sit on his lap at all. The spirit of lust knows no boundaries. We cannot invite the devil inside and then set up boundaries. That's like sitting in a tub full of water and expecting not to get wet.

Utterly impossible!

Anyways, the confusion continued throughout my childhood up until my teenage years. People outside of our household thought my father was so cool. *Go figure.* They thought he was so giving, and truth be told, he was with them. He also definitely threw his money at women around us and he helped his friends, or for better words, "our fake aunties." He barely gave my mother money for our needs. Only time I received money from him was when he was drunk and generous. Then, he would give a few bucks to me and my friends. I went from being embarrassed to actually waiting for a Friday or Saturday night to see him drunk again only because my friends liked him. Of course, the few extra bucks didn't hurt.

He was a real social bug as well. Mommy tells me 'til this day that I am like him in that way because I am able to communicate with everyone. However, those other habits started to grow deep inside of me. I began to steal his favorite bottle of whiskey. Let's be real, he didn't keep alcohol around much, but this particular bottle was gifted to him, so he saved it. Well, I opened it. I began to take some out and refill the bottle with water. Later, he discovered it and I made up some lie about me being so upset by his drinking that I poured it out to prevent him from getting intoxicated.

That was a pure lie.

I was about 14 years old, partaking in a bottle of expensive apple flavored whiskey. I absolutely hated the taste, but I did it to get back at him. *Does that even make sense? Hurt myself in order to hurt him? Probably not.* Oh well, I still did it. I wanted to feel like he did. I wanted to enjoy the most important thing to him, a cold drink!

After I drank that, I began to get bold enough to walk into the liquor stores right in my area. I didn't have to show off any type of ID. The owners only cared about their money and killing our people. I would buy Saint Ides and Old English. Sometimes, I would challenge the boys on the block to a drink off and most times I won. Then, I began to throw up.

The last draw for me was when I brought that poison to school one day. My friends loved my boldness and they also enjoyed drinking. That day, I drank too much and fell down the steps. Everyone that was important saw me and I was so embarrassed. I was almost busted by the teachers, until I made up a story about getting dizzy and having cramps. The office allowed me to lay down and recover on the floor. I never brought alcohol to school after that. I also calmed down with the drinking. One thing I didn't want to be was an embarrassing drunk. Needless to say, this was the first of many bad traits I acted out in memory of my father.

CHAPTER TWO: THE LOSING FIGHT

Out of everything that we endured with my father, I never hated him. I always loved him – at least until the hate crept in.

"What does he have? Stop lying, no he doesn't! Who told you? You know?"

These were the words that I expressed to my middle brother after he broke the news to me. My brother was angry at my father for a number of reasons, so this was nothing new, but the rage in his eyes was pure hate! When I tell you, "when it rains it pours," this is an understatement. I was totally in awe! Nothing could ever prepare me for this. My mouth was on the floor.

So, this was why my father was so sick and in and out of the hospital. My once fully-figured, masculine father, who was extremely handsome, was now the size of a Slim Jim. He had sores all over his ears that were full of blisters and pus. He had open scabs all over his scalp. Not to mention all the dead skin left on the toilet bowl seat after he used it. It was a purely gross sight to see.

I remember thinking, *Oh, please don't blow dry your hair again, it smells like burning flesh.*

Every time I would use the bathroom, I would have to reclean everything now.

Lord Jesus don't hug me again, I would think. It was amazing how he wanted to give out hugs now.

So many thoughts would go through my mind.

Your nasty, bloody ear lobe touched my face! I am about to pass out! I cannot deal with this anymore! I absolutely hate going home. I can't even tell anybody. What will my friends think of me...of us? Oh, my goodness! MY MOTHER!

Did he give my mother a death sentence? Did he just kill my saved, Holy Ghost-filled, and fire-baptized mother? My mother, who loves the Lord. My mother, who has been committed to God since she was 14 years old. Who married as a virgin? My mother, who cared for us all. My mother, who loved my father even through his cheating, even when she walked in on him and this white woman in our home!

All the lies and deception! My mother, who loves us all unconditionally. This mother!? Did you just kill my mother? You fucking bum! I hope you die and go to HELL with gasoline draws on! I know for sure Mommy will divorce you now!

So, I thought. *Joke's on me.*

What does he have again? He has Herpes! What else does he have? He has...he has...he really has AIDS?! What about mommy?" He said they don't know yet. That's ok Momma, you keep loving him. I have enough hate for the both of us. Yes, you heard right. I will hate him for you. Preserve your soul Momma. He is as good as dead to me!

I know it seems like I am making my father out to be a huge monster. You have to understand, to a child, who once adored her dad and feared him, he now became someone I had no respect for. Truth be told, my father never did anything that wowed me. He never treated me so amazingly with love, gifts, and admiration – nothing of the sorts.

However, according to my mother, he never left us. Most times, I wished he had. Besides the occasional hitting I endured from my youngest brother, the emotional coldness of my middle brother, oh and the lack of interest I received from my oldest brother, life was decent. Of course, my brothers thought I was a spoiled brat – more like a bitch in their eyes. Well, you just try being the youngest of five.

You have no voice with anyone, from your parents to your siblings, who tell you what to do. It's amazing how I never disrespected my dad to his face. There was no such thing as talking back or even giving him the evil eye. Had I done that, I wouldn't be breathing today. So, I never fully understood the severity of his punishments toward any of us. I don't fault my brothers for the way they treated me because I figured most little sisters got treated cruel and are made fun of by their siblings.

Hey, I figured that everyone got real fish heads cut off and put in their clothing drawers. Maybe even tormented their little sisters with food, and made songs about how they couldn't hold much food because they had a sensitive stomach. Oh yes, my siblings made a song about me, and I remember every word of it.

It went a little something like this:

> **"Angie got a brown tooth,**
> **a line on her nose,**
> **a little tiny stomach,**
> **and a moley toe."**

Yup! That's the song.

My youngest brother had terrible temper issues. He was diagnosed as Emotionally Disturbed. At that time, I didn't understand what that meant. So, needless to say, I was always defending myself against his evil ways. At one point, it got so bad that me and another friend of mine plotted to kill him. The plan was to lure him into the park and shoot him with my friend's father's gun. We were going to leave him for dead.

However, God gave me a dream about him – like he often did when we were not on speaking terms. The Lord must have given me over 15 dreams of reconciliation with my brother because anything sparked an outrage with him. Yet, if anything happened to him, I would go bananas. Oh, no one said I was a saint. I just wasn't a bully, but my youngest brother was that and so much more. I could ask him a simple question about eating my food, taking my money, or stealing my belongings, and he would turn his wrath upon me.

One day, when he hit me in my face, I fell to the floor screaming, and I actually called the police for the first time in my life. He never hit me again after they took him to jail. He only stayed for a day or two, but that also taught him that his home would be behind bars if he ever touched me again. Unfortunately, his angry streak continued on, just not with me. In his defense, he would whoop anybody's ass if they messed with me, but I believe that was the rule for dysfunctional families. Yeah, we are fucked up, but don't fuck with either one of us.

Just thinking about my brothers. Hell, they even went so far as to prank me to eat dog poop. They told me it was a goddamn cookie! That was some bullshit if I ever heard any. I got my mouth good and ready to bite on a "white powdered donut" off the ground, persuaded by the people I trusted with my life. Now that I think about it, that was such an evil prank that I fell for. Thankfully, my youngest brother slapped it out of my hand before I sunk my teeth into it. The stories revolving around them are endless.

I didn't feel bad all the times they got in trouble because, 9 times out of ten, I'm the one who told on them. My father would light them up! I'm pretty sure that may have made their hearts turn cold against me even more. I knew my father was strict and excessive, so there were things he would not go for. He didn't like hearing a bunch of noise, he didn't like calling us more than once, and he didn't like ***REBELLIOUS AND DISOBEDIENT*** children. His remedy for everything above was – take a guess – a beating. What he failed to realize was that we all reacted differently to his harsh treatment. My brothers became extremely angry and resentful.

When my brothers were younger, they would get jumped by gangs of people at once. Sometimes, they even ran home from school because they weren't safe anywhere. This went on for years. My oldest brother turned to lifting weights, so he got so big that no one dared to mess with him. My middle brother was right behind him, but my middle brother was scary. Scary in the sense that no one could figure him out. He was very quiet at times and he grew angry in his demeanor. Nonetheless, he was very intimidating.

My father withheld his love and affection for his three sons when he should have graced them with it, especially seeing as though they were being mistreated by others. Indirectly, it was as if all three of them were trying to prove their strength to everyone they came in contact with.

My middle brother had a look so stern that, if you looked at him too long, you would be the first to turn away. In high school, he took up wrestling and received several awards from it. It was good for him because he released a lot of anger on those mats and on his opponents. Don't get it wrong though, my father was still to be feared by us all, so we dared not confront him. Oh, but there was one of us crazy enough to do just that – my youngest brother, Nat.

At this point, he didn't care. My father had kicked him out of the house because he dropped out of school when he was 18 years old. Let's be honest, he never fully stayed gone, he just wasn't allowed back in the house until after school was over. One day, my father told my brother to clean the leaves in the yard, and my brother did that. Then, he had more work for him to do, and when he told my brother to do that work, Nat refused. He told my father that if he told him to do anything else he was going to kick his ass. That was comical seeing as though my brother was so arrogant and headstrong that he really thought he could fight my dad. Before you knew it, my father made another demand when he walked back into the house where my brother was.

"Nathaniel, get out here and skin this fish, and after that I have something else for you to do!"

Now, why did my dad have to go and say that? Next thing I knew, my brother flew past me with magical powers and started swinging on my dad! The door was still wide open. I don't know if any of those punches actually landed though. All I remember was my father grabbing, punching, and kicking my brother down the steps, eventually. Then, he kicked my brother in the face with his cowboy boots. Of course, I was in the background screaming! My brother got back up, but my father locked the door. My mother tried to break up the fight and received many bruises. In fact, my mother intervened in a lot of the fights between my two youngest brothers that left her with black and blue marks all over her body. This particular time, my father told my brother he couldn't come back inside. My oldest brother came home after the fight was over, and my middle brother had already made his escape from the family when he went away to college a while before.

Oh yeah, let me tell you about my oldest brother. My oldest brother was into women – much like our father. He was very handsome as well. Thus, he looked a lot like our father. I can't imagine the pressure of growing up and trying to be perfect for my father because he was the mini version of him. The pressure to make him happy must have been overwhelming. On top of that, the responsibility to care for his younger siblings. That's a lot of responsibility, combined with the abuse and lack of attention and love from our father.

On the other hand, my mother was *full* of love and adoration, so she gave it in abundance. However, nothing makes up for the love of a father. That validation was simply lacking. Do you know the feeling of a little boy who looked up to his dad, but never received what he was in search of? The weight of that rejection and abandonment is real. Eventually, he began to act out in one form or another. That feeling of low self-esteem grew with his age, but before he knew it, Ty was a ladies' mane. Yes, he made his own money, so he didn't have time to be home with all the chaos and dysfunction. He went to school, worked, and stayed out as much as possible. I remember when he finally got a car. He became more of a magnet for the women.

My father definitely sowed those seeds. It seemed that he taught his sons that being a man was to use their sexuality. He even told them to protect themselves, which is something he didn't do himself. He shared stories with them about women he was with and regretted. I remember one time my brother had his friends in their room watching pornography. I pushed myself inside to see what they were doing and I saw it. I saw a few people having sex on the television and I called myself running to tell my dad. Then, he ran into the room and a few seconds later he came running out. I rejoiced knowing my brothers were busted! However, my dad ran back into the room only to put on his glasses, as if he were trying to get a better look. My dad did not even come back out of the room until the video ended.

Unbelievable!

My middle brother started out the timidest out of the other two. He was actually the only brother I enjoyed and felt like he was the nicest. Although all my brothers played games and tricks on me, it didn't appear as harsh as the treatment from my oldest and youngest brothers. However, the tolerance level and aggression of my middle brother grew more and more abrasive. It was clear that he wasn't happy either. The one I went to when I was attacked by my youngest brother was now the one who turned a cold shoulder or just seemed like he didn't care.

You see, my father called us all names. He was verbally abusive to all of his children. God only knows how many times I was called a "Nigger." I was called stupid, retarded, dumb, and so many other names. My other siblings endured that harsh treatment as well. My middle brother was called things like a sissy, and a girl all because he didn't fight and cried too much for my father's liking. That dynamic changed over the years though. It seemed as if all that talking down to him made him cold, numb, broken, angry, and far from a punk.

Instead of being jumped, now my brothers were part of the jumps. Just know, whenever someone stepped to my brothers, they were ready this time. They were no longer push overs or the ones who turned the other cheek and ran. They embraced the black eyes and bruises just as long as it meant they fought back. It had even gotten to a point where my two youngest brothers didn't get along and had many fights. The anger built up so much in them both that they didn't even realize that they were fighting the wrong person.

If they could only run to my father and tell him how they felt. If only they could share with him the pain that he had embarked upon them for all these years. Maybe, they would have received an answer or maybe he would finally tell them that he really loved them. Maybe let them know the real reason why he treated them that way was because he hated himself. Maybe, he could have told them that he was lost and broken from not having his own father in his life.

I realized in my adult years that my father could not give us what he did not have himself. He did what he knew how to do as a father. Whether it was right or wrong, he gave what he had. There was something in each one of us that must have triggered the child inside my father. His first bet was to always beat the innocence out of us. Keep in mind, all children start out innocent. There is something that happens to pollute them and their ways of acting, thinking, and behaving.

However, there are no perfect children just like there are no perfect parents. How we would give anything to hear our father tell us just one proud word. It was like it was painful for him to do. I'm sure my father was in a lot of pain, but he just never shared with us – he definitely never shared it with me. Explaining anything to a child was taboo, especially with a country boy from Georgia.

My father was one of eight children. His father left his mother for another woman, so he didn't get to have a life with two parents. Instead, he lived a hard life. People would say, "At least he didn't leave y'all like his father abandoned him," but I prayed so many times that my father would leave. As a child, I thought that we would be better with my mother alone. However, that never happened. At least until the day he took his last breath...

At that point, my middle brother was away at college for about a year and he only came back for the funeral. When he left, we were not on speaking terms. He disowned me after a ridiculous argument over the remote control. I had been watching television before my brother came into the living room with his friend. I left for a moment and when I returned, they were there. I picked up the remote control to finish what I was watching when my brother snatched it out of my hand. I went to grab it again and told him I was watching it first. However, he was very abrupt and confrontational. He called me a bitch and threatened me in front of his friend. Then, he told me to go and cry about it like I always do. I walked away and was embarrassed.

The next day, I made an attempt to talk to him, but he just looked at me. Several days later, he told me never to speak to him again. Two years had passed before we spoke words to one another again. It didn't matter to me though because I disliked who he had become. Out of the blue, he invited me to come visit him at his college. I was illuminated! I agreed, went to see him, and the rest is history. Years later, he apologized for that terrible encounter. He promised me that it wasn't anything I did to provoke that reaction and that he was angry about the life we lived there at the house.

Yes, I was a brat, and yes, my brothers enjoyed it when I got into trouble because, for some reason, they thought I got away with everything. What they didn't see was me serving my father on a daily basis. When the oldest siblings were gone, I was left to do it all. I had to clean, do light cooking, and do whatever my father asked me to do. This included going to the store several times a day. I remember telling my father that I was not a slave, and because my sister was sick, she couldn't help. She wasn't able to do as much as I could. When she was well, she had her daughter to tend to, and if she wasn't taking care of her, she was out with her boyfriend. My oldest brother was at school, then at work, so I rarely saw him. When he was around, my dad had them doing outside work. The inside work was for us girls. My middle brother was home for a while but also got a job with my oldest brother. Eventually, he also went to college.

 My youngest brother was a rebel. He rebelled against everything and everyone. He became a bully not only to me but to his and my friends. It was like he wanted to hurt people before they hurt him. He was very mischievous and he enjoyed getting himself into all types of evil activities. He also liked the girls. He had a child in his teenage years just like my sister.

 My point is, I was left home every day, to deal with being my father's slave. He actually told me that's why I was born. My existence was to serve my father, and because of this, I resented him more and more. I rebelled, not in action, but in thoughts and in my heart. I detested the way my father made me feel like less than a person. I never received encouraging words or anything positive from my father.

 If my mother bought anything for me, he would tell her that I didn't need it. He withheld money for our needs *constantly*. My mother decided it was best for her to get a job in order to care for us. My brothers have stories of wearing hand-me-downs or clothes that were too small. Even when my father would buy sneakers for my brothers and me, they would be cheap and eventually fall apart. Sometimes, our feet would grow out of them.

 My father withheld his finances because he didn't feel or see the need to give us *new* things. My middle brother has a story of putting cardboard on the bottom of his sneakers because he had a hole in them. The other kids said there was a smell coming from those same sneakers. *Shame.* No parents should ever subject their children to these conditions if they can control them. As a parent, your job is to protect as well as provide for them. They didn't ask to be here.

 I had lost all respect for my father. Of course, I never talked back or approached my father about things I didn't like because I just dealt with them. Sometimes, I also told my mother. My father's other argument was that he did not like wasteful children either and that's what we were to him. If we had a plate of food and it was full, there was no throwing it away. If you didn't finish it, he had a good ole belt just waiting for you with your name on it. Sometimes, I could not finish my food and went to throw it up. I also received a spanking for throwing up the food.

You have to understand that I honored my father. So, if I didn't do exactly what he said, not only would I be punished, but my father would give me the silent treatment. We would go days in silence. He would just tell me what to do and that was it. He avoided any conversation except to direct me to do things or chores. Because of this, I learned what it was like to be silent in anger. I grew a nasty disposition, and I held grudges like nobody's business. Hey, I learned it from the best. If you pissed me off, we could be face to face and I operated like you were invisible. This kind of sick behavior is taught, and this type of behavior continued for years, especially after he knew that the children found out about his illness.

He despised me even more. This time, I cringed at the thought of being in the same room with him and he could feel it. Sometimes, after school, I would come home hungry, and ask him for something to eat. I remember him saying to me," So what! What are you telling me for?"

I was shocked.

At times, my father would be lying across the couch when I came home from school. On the top of the couch, he lined up all kinds of cakes and all sorts of potato chips. This particular day, he had a can of Dinty Moore Beef Stew just looking at me. So, I swallowed my spit and built up the courage to ask him for it. I also added, "I'm asking you because you're my father."

He looked at me with nine eyes and told me to shut up and stop trying to be so smart. I told him that was not what I was doing, but I was hungry and there was nothing to eat. I asked him for the soup again, and he ignored me. I asked again and he told me to get from in front of the TV. I remembered that I stormed out crying. About ten minutes later, he called me back into the living room and handed me the can of soup. I told him thank you and rushed to go make it. It was the best soup I ever had!

We were not poor. My father had a good job, but he definitely didn't do all the right things with his money by not buying his family a house when the opportunity came. He also partied a lot and spent money on his whores. Some of them wrote letters to my mother telling her she was stupid for staying with him. Some of them we knew as our "aunts." That was a lie! My father had enough money to take care of the needs of us all when he did the right things. So, he could have bought some food or even sent me to the store. His coldness and lack of concern has always concerned me. Until this day, most of my questions lay unanswered.

  We didn't live in the suburbs, but we didn't live in the heart of the hood either. We were in the urban part where everyone's parents were hard-working men and women who took care of their properties. Now, the first place we lived in was on a busy avenue. Then, my father moved us to this building that was on the corner in the hood. It was a really bad area and the school system wasn't the best. The children who lived there were a product of their environment like we were. However, my aunt, who is my father's sister, owned a rental house, and we moved in there. That apartment was everything to us, even though I had to share a room with my sister. We lived across the street from the park that we had gone to all of our lives. In our eyes, we had moved on up.

  I'm sorry to paint a picture of my father as this huge monster that tried to eat us up all day and all night. My memories of those good times were few. Some good memories I have were when we had wonderful family picnics that his job would give. Also, we had wonderful cookouts on specific holidays, such as the Fourth of July, at my uncle's house in Morristown. He would always make homemade ice cream, and we would eat watermelons and other good foods. When we went fishing, we had loads of fun. That was until one day, I wasn't invited. I guess it was a boy's outing only. There was also this lake we would go and ride boats once a year. Those times were really fun.

  Unfortunately, I don't hold too many of those memories. As time went on, life for me grew colder and colder.

CHAPTER THREE: LIFE IS FOR THE LIVING

Still to this day, I have had to learn to make a conscious decision to let things go. There were so many unanswered questions about my father's love...the lack of it...the dysfunction behind it... the question of whether it was even love at all? When I did ask my father, moreso towards the end of his life, he never answered. He just looked at me like I was crazy. I would argue with myself and scream at him, asking him, "Why do you treat me this way?" He never answered. Basically, what was... was.

One day, when I see him in heaven, I will know. As an adult, I now understand much more than I ever could, even if he answered me. To live life and to be presented with the same issues as all other people trying to live for Christ, you realize the real adversary. I realized those same demons that once haunted my father knew my address too. They were in my house, and they were in my face. They were operating in my life and were not going to stop until I gave in because they were coming for my soul. *Had it not been for the prayers of the righteous, where would I be?* It is so easy to give in to the flesh and all of its evil desires. It's much harder to try to do the right thing. The devil isn't really on your back when you're doing what he wants. The moment you decide to live for Christ is the moment he comes to kill, steal, and destroy your very being. You have to put on the whole armor of God in order to live a life without defeat. You can't afford to relax, and you can't afford to think – even for a moment – that you have overcome every situation because you passed a few tests. The second you fall asleep, just know the enemy is plotting their next attack.

In the midst of coming out of one battle with my father, here I was, faced with another blow. When I opened up my eyes, I expected to be in Heaven. My father and I had some kind of issue that, once again, left me clueless. I was clueless as to why he couldn't love me. He left me confused, wondering why my mistakes made me less worthy of his love.

At this point, my father only spoke a few words to me. I wasn't a child who talked back and forth to my father. So, I had not treated him any differently. At the age of 12, I had not yet found out about his disease to question him about it. Even after that, I was always a child who did what I was told or else reap the consequences. In my family, there was no such thing as tell your parents what was on your mind, especially not to my father. So, I struggled with the rejection from my dad. I didn't know how to please this man.

"Why don't he love me?!" I used to ask myself with so much hurt and despair in my heart.

My mother assured me he did, but he just didn't know how to show it.

One day, he gave me a card for my birthday. Inside the card was a message saying that he loved me. When I asked him if he really loved me, he squeezed his fingers and told me only a little bit. So, I asked him about how much. He told me that he only loved me up to the streetlights. If you grew up in urban areas, you had lights on every block that you would call the " streetlights." They would come on just before it got dark. Our parents would tell us to be inside the house before the lights came on. Of course, we tried to stay out later, but if those lights came on, we were prepared to be in trouble. These lights weren't that tall because they stood about the same height as a house.

My father told me that was the extent of his love for me.
Wow!

My feelings were so hurt, but he didn't care because he would walk away laughing. Then, I would express my feelings to my mother. She would tell me that he didn't mean it, but my heart knew better. It literally pained my father to tell me he loved me.

"Angie, Angie, wake up!" My mother kept making attempts to shake me. "Angie, please wake up! Erving, Angie will not wake up!"

"She is just sleeping. What's wrong with her?" my dad asked.

As my mother moved me, she picked up the two bottles of pills that came from underneath me. All I could hear in the background was her calling my father's name and telling him to call the ambulance. I finally woke up. My mother kept asking me what I take, but I kept drifting back out. I told her that I didn't want to live anymore. The next thing I remember is my father picking me up and putting me in the back seat of the car.

I woke up in the hospital. My body must have been having a bad reaction to the medicine I had taken because it caused my body to jolt and gyrate. I remember one of the male nurses telling me that I was beautiful. He asked me why I would want to kill myself? He told me that the Lord loved me and that I wouldn't want to open up my eyes in HELL had my attempt been successful. He had taken out many young bodies inside of body bags, so he made me promise never to try that again. Out of nowhere, I began to throw up. The nurse told me that it was good to throw up because that meant they didn't have to pump out my stomach. After I felt a little better, my mother and I had to sit in an office with a counselor, who then called a mental hospital in another town. However, as the counselor spoke with the director at "the midnight hour," they couldn't find an empty bed. The director also didn't want to wake up and do paperwork, so they made my mother promise to look after me.

They asked me a few questions that I answered. I assured them I would not do it again and that I did it to get away from my father. My mother was praying the entire time. I knew that was what tied the enemy's hands. There was power in her prayers to the Lord. Luckily, my father was waiting outside in the car and was nowhere in sight.

When we arrived home, I went back to bed. I remember that I did not go to school for the next couple of days because I needed to rest. My body had those convulsions for the next few days. I remember my mother giving me a Hershey's candy bar to help me cope. As I drifted in and out of sleep, I would eat a piece of it. In the days to come, my brothers started looking at me weirdly and asking me questions, but then it kind of went away as if it never happened. From that point on, I just existed – still, my father spoke no words.

My father would line us up with our hands, palm side up, to get spanked sometimes when he didn't know which of us were guilty. *Talk about guilty by association!* Sometimes, when the older siblings were responsible for the younger, we got in trouble. Then, we all received a spanking. It was more than a few licks per hand. We better not move at all...*or else!* That lasted all childhood until I was about 13 years old.

With every strike, he screamed and yelled words. "YOU-BET-NOT-EVER-DO-THAT-AGAIN-OR-I'M-GONNA-WHOOP-YOUR TAIL!" Then, he continued with his stutter saying, "NOW-DID-N'T-I-TELL-YOU-TO-CLEAN-UP-THAT-KITCHEN-BEFORE-YOU-WATCHED-TV? I'M-SICK-AND-TIRED-OF-TELLING-YOU-THE-SAME-THING-EVERY-SINGLE-DAY!"

The list goes on and on. At one point, it got so that we knew exactly what he was going to say. One thing I did know was that a whopping was never funny. It was only funny to watch someone else – sometimes. I remember knocking on the wall to my father's room, since he didn't have a door, and telling about something my brother did to me or someone else. Before you knew it, he either had me go get my brother, or he would storm out himself. Most times, he sent me to get my brother. Majority of the time, my brother wouldn't come at my command, which meant he got in even more trouble because he made my father get up from watching one of his shows or resting.

All you would hear from my youngest brother was screaming! My dad would also spank my oldest two brothers. Naturally, my brothers would run and try their best to protect and cover up their limbs. Unfortunately, once my father got to you, that was a wrap. Just practice holding your breath until it is over.

When we got spanked by my mother, she would forget sometimes and we would be so relieved. Then, after about two days had passed, she would approach you and tell you that she didn't forget about the promised spanking. She would tell us to prepare ourselves to get a beating after school that day. Now, I would be tormented the entire school day waiting for three o'clock to come. I would take the longest time getting home those days. Sometimes, I would fall asleep before she came home from work. Unlike my father, who would completely forget if we fell asleep, my mother would wake us up. The rest is history.

CHAPTER FOUR: THE LAST DRAW

One day in August, I was 14 years old and had just finished ninth grade. My mother allowed me to go to North Carolina for the summer. I had such a wonderful time there that when I came back home, I wished I could go back to stay there. No way my parents were allowing that to happen, but at the end of the summer, something happened that changed my life forever.

It was late in the afternoon when my mother told me to do something. I was going to do it; however, I was in the middle of doing something else in my room. Instead of me stopping to tend to what my mother wanted me to do, I finished up what I was doing.. After I finished, I got up, went to the door, and opened it to walk out. There was my father. He looked at me angrily and yelled, "WHY DIDN'T YOU DO WHAT YOUR MOTHER TOLD YOU TO DO WHEN SHE ASKED YOU TO DO IT!"

Scared as hell, I replied, "I was going to do it. I was on my way after I finished up in my room."

Clearly, I didn't move fast enough. My father debated with what I was saying and told me he was sick of my rebellious ways and disobedience. He told me he was going to give me a whooping. Here I am, 14 years old – soon to be 15 – and this man thought he was about to give me a whopping. He wouldn't even allow my mother to have a say so.

I don't know what got into me, but I was determined to defend myself this time. I must have watched one too many female superhero movies because I felt super powerful. So much so, that for the first time , I had told myself that I was going to defend myself at all costs. In my head, the scenario went a lot differently than what actually happened in reality.

My father came into my room with a belt in his hands. I jumped up on the bed and threw a few plastic hangers at him. Those same plastic hangers bounced off of him like a penny would. They had no effect on him at all. Then , he grabbed me and began to beat me with the belt. I fell off the bed, so he began to beat on the back of my neck with the belt. I tried to cover my entire body, but it was no use. I was screaming for my mother, who then called for my oldest brother to help get my father off of me. I remember seeing both, my brother and mother at the door. The only thing was that my brother would not let my mother through the door to help me. He blocked her from helping me, so I continued to scream. Finally, my brother moved and grabbed my father.

At that point, my father was already done. He shoved my brother and told him to get off of him. Then, my mother came to my aid. I screamed at my brother for not allowing my mother to help me. At that moment, my brother was my biggest enemy. *How could he watch his baby sister get pounded on that way? So much so, that the back of my neck was bleeding, and my body was covered with whelps.*

He said to me, "Yea, that's what your spoiled brat butt gets! Now you know how it feels!" he said, chuckling as he walked out.

The fact that my brother actually took delight in the abuse that took place right before his eyes bothered me immensely. He could never protect me after that and I never came to him for refuge after that event. I learned to trust in strangers before my own blood.

My father came back just to say, "I beat you for OLD AND NEW! All the things that you thought you got away with, now I made up for. OLD AND NEW! If anybody tell you to do anything, you better do it or it will be worse than that!"

My immediate response to my mother was, "What are we gonna do now?"

My mother didn't understand the question. "Momma, I'm a young lady now. If you sit here and allow Daddy to beat me with my brother watching, you are condoning domestic violence." I gave her the most serious look. "If you do nothing, you are programming me to take abuse from other men. I refuse to stay in this house anymore."

I gave her one option. Let me move to the South with her best friend and her daughters or I would runway. Ultimately, my mother took me down to the police station, where I actually pressed charges on my father. He found out later when he received the letter in the mail stating what day he had to go to court. He was upset with my mother, and I was upset with the world.

When my mother first told me that I could not go to live down South, I started to rebel all the more. I remember when I tore the pages out of the Holy Bible and cursed the day I was born. I actually thought I could curse God! I cursed everyone in my family!

I WANTED OUT! I NEEDED OUT!

Because of all the chaos and lack of peace in the house, eventually, my mother allowed me to go live in North Carolina with her friend and her daughters for a while. So, she gave her temporary custody of me. I remember sitting in front of a judge answering a bunch of questions. Next thing I knew, I was gone. That was the Last Draw for me.

Life can teach you a great deal of lessons. Just when you think you are escaping one bad situation, you find yourself in another. If you don't deal with those demons at home, they do nothing short of follow you wherever you go. I wasn't healed, free, or happy when I left. The change of environment gave me a false sense of safety and pleasure. Now, I entered a whole other realm. I was unleashed to the real evil realities of life. I was no longer under my father's roof. Thus, I was free – so it seemed.

Yes, a lot of bad things had already happened in my life. I hadn't exactly had a 5-star childhood experience, but I did have a father. I did have someone watching over my soul, even if he played a part in contaminating it. I went to another atmosphere with nothing, but women. No man, no father, basically, no male leadership anywhere. If you think for a moment there isn't a difference without male intervention in a home, you are sadly mistaken. Take away the covering, and you are left naked. You're wide-open for the wolves to take you as their own. I would soon learn the error of my ways, and how cold and cruel this world really can be. Without the known coverage and protection I had all my life, my mind, body, and soul was about to experience something I wasn't ready for. Something far worse than I could have ever imagined.

There is an order within the home that some people don't want to admit to. Of course, women are meant to take on leadership roles within their homes when there is an absence of a man. However, if you are a believer in Christ and follow principles in the Bible, you would understand that God created man to protect and lead his family. Anytime it goes contrary to that, there will be all manners of confusion, division, and strife.

My father started out following Christ. Then, the issues of life overtook him and he became unhappy within himself. Whatever state my father was in, he still remained my father. He still provided us with a roof over our heads, and he still never left us. The lack of love that my family received from my father should not have dictated the respect we, as children, gave him. He was still the head of the household. The bible didn't tell us to honor and obey him if he treated us well. It commanded us to honor our parents so our days would be longer. I had to learn that I was not my parents' judge and jury. My only responsibility was to obey them, whether they were right or wrong. Unfortunately, some of us had to learn the hard way. As I stated before, I never disobeyed my father, but in my heart, I hated him because of his harsh treatment towards me. I suffered more emotional abuse than I did physical. I couldn't wait to turn 18 years old so I could do whatever I wanted. I was rebellious. At some point, I wanted to do what I wanted to do. My spirit opposed anything I was told to do by my father.

Why should I do anything for a man who keeps trying to control me? A man who treats me like a slave. A man who didn't know how to be a father. A man who lacked compassion. A man who treated me like a robot. My father, who never told me that he loved me. What child believes that the Lord Jesus Christ loves them, when their earthly father gives them none? It's extremely hard to believe. Besides, didn't the Lord allow this abuse? Doesn't he know what will happen beforehand? Isn't he all-knowing and all-wise? Then, how could a God who knows all of that allow terrible things to happen to us all? I had to learn through a lot of long suffering, patience, forgiveness, and deliverance that God was for me. He had been there with me through it all. In every hurt, every pain, every illness, every hardship, and every burden—He was there. Always. I had to learn that not one ounce of what I went through would go to waste, but that he could use it all for his glory. Something beautiful could and would be made out of this mess called "my life."

So many times, I would wish my life away. I wish I had never been born. At times, I wished I belonged to another family. I also vowed to run away from guys who were anything like my father – even those like my brothers. Of course, I was attracted to men; however, my perception of love was defiled at a young age. The confusion between my mother and father about what was holy and what was carnal played on my mind.

My father went to church sometimes, while my mother went often and raised us attending Sunday School. We attended church every Sunday, for choir and dance practices, and for Vacation Bible School over the Summer breaks. My dad was in a different multicultural ministry than us, so he went to church at night. I remember eating a grape out of the hands of W.V. Grant. I also remembered seeing my father preach at times in those churches. He would call himself Rev. E.L. Mitchell and he would write notebooks full of sermons. I, too, wanted to be a preacher because I admired the preacher's zeal and love of the Lord.

However, it started to get harder and harder to understand why Daddy would reek with the smell of alcohol. It was hard to see him stumbling in the house on a weekend or whatever day he had off from work. It was confusing to see him sleep all day when we knew he should have been up praying or even attending church on a Sunday. Instead, he had to sleep off being sick from drinking too much.

You start to get the concept that you can do both – live any kind of way, and still serve the Lord. Sometimes, Daddy would be so sick, his stomach would hurt, and he would want me to pray for him. He told me I was the only one who could make him feel better. So, I would get the Holy oil, place it on his stomach, and pray. He promised me that I would make it all better. That prayer lasted from 5 years old until I turned 8 years old. Then, he never asked me again.

Those times were the only times I felt connected to him. I actually felt like he needed me then. I remember eagerly anticipating praying for his tummy aches again. I would feel like it was my purpose to help him in those moments of vulnerability. The act of praying, even at such a young age, gave me a sense of control over a situation that seemed chaotic and beyond my control. It was as if I could bring some peace to the turmoil that constantly surrounded him and my family.

When those moments stopped, it left a void that I couldn't fill. It was as if the connection we had was severed, and I was left with the daunting realization that my role in his life was never what I thought it was. The person I once thought I could heal became unreachable. Then, I began to understand that love isn't enough to fix the brokenness in someone else. It was a painful lesson that would stay with me for many years.

CHAPTER FIVE: INNOCENCE LOST

We learned about God more than most of my friends, so much so that they would call me "Church Girl." It's funny because, looking back and knowing what I do now, that was a compliment. I even tried my hardest to prove to my friends that it wasn't true. I could be just as vile and profane as they were. In some cases, even more. Honestly, I sought the approval of my friends growing up. It's a dangerous place to be in when you feel the need to look for validation within people who don't know or care to know the ways of the Lord. My validation should have come from the Lord alone.

To have two parents in the home, yet only one who could pay attention or give me the love I longed for, only made me seek love elsewhere. It felt like, in the eyes of my father, I could do no good. I was never noticed for anything, even though I was good in school and made the Honor Roll often. I took pride in being smart, but I started acting out in the 5th grade. My issues at home began to seep into my academics and behavior at school. So, the teachers began to call home. That year, I stayed in trouble. I even stuck my middle finger up at my teacher. When my mother was notified, I received the beating of my lifetime. Needless to say, I straightened up and didn't recall having any more serious issues until the 11th grade.

At that point, I was now living, temporarily, in North Carolina, with my extended family. I had grown up with my mother's best friend's daughters, mostly all my life. The middle daughter was my best friend at that time. I absolutely adored being with them, although me and the daughter next to the youngest daughter always fought. We both were strong-willed and swore on our very lives that we knew it all. I was extremely bossy, and well, she was just always seeking attention. I wanted my best friend to myself, and she acted like we just had to include her in just about everything we did. We fought like cats and dogs. Honestly, she actually fought with everyone that way.

Nevertheless, I loved it there. Although their mother was excessively strict, she always treated me with kindness. She allowed me to come to her home whenever I wanted. She was always at work as well, so her daughters and I got into all kinds of trouble. We stole candy from the stores, we ate what we wanted, and we played all kinds of games. Sometimes, we would have company over to the house, and other times we went out when we shouldn't have. Clearly, we didn't have that much supervision.

After some time passed, I began to talk to this handsome young man who was about four years older than me. He lived in the complex a few blocks over. One day, this young man asked me to hold this bag for him. He made me promise to hold it just for a few days. Those few days eventually turned into a couple of weeks. Out of curiosity, I looked inside the bag, and what I saw was about 30-40 little bags of marijuana. When the end of the second week came, I told him I could no longer keep holding it for him because my best friend kept asking about it. So, he came and picked it up sooner than he had expected to. Two days later, he got locked up for illegal possession of drugs. I never spoke with him again.

Not too long afterwards, I was introduced to this beautiful teenager who lived down the street. She was a good friend to my best friend and she was a few years older than us. She was about to turn 18 years old and was a senior in high school. She would practice doing our hair for free because she was really good.

One day, I went over to her house with my best friend so we could hang out. Her handsome father came home from work, and I could tell he took a liking to me because he started flirting with me. I felt awkward at first, but then I began to enjoy the little remarks he made. As beautiful as I had been told I was, I really didn't believe it. *If I was, why didn't my father see this beauty enough to love me?*

Anyways, I couldn't wait to go back to visit her again, and that's exactly what I did. A few days later, she invited me over, so I went. To my surprise, her uncle, her father's 28 year old brother, was there. If I thought her father was handsome, then her uncle was drop-dead gorgeous. This man looked like Al B. Sure! I knew nothing about dealing with older men. Of course, they hit on me or would talk slick back home in Jersey, but I would talk slick right back and told them to *FUCK OFF*! They would call me all types of bitches, but I didn't care. I would just keep it moving. If anything, it was a turn-off.

Now, this fully grown man was looking at me in a way I had not experienced. I thought to myself that this southern hospitality was on another level than up North. My friend told him to leave me alone. She didn't know who was worse, him, or her father. Briefly, I told him who I was and where I came from. Then, I asked him his age and he told me he was 28 years old. I was shocked because he definitely looked much younger. He told me his older brother was too old for me because he was 38. He was clearly old enough to be my father. He assured me that age meant nothing in the South. My friends were also dealing with older men, so 10 years older was nothing to them. I didn't see that much up North – at least not in the open.

As we kept talking, I noticed that the hour was getting late. My friend ended up walking me home halfway. Before I left, her uncle asked me if I could come see him the next day. I assured him that I would. I couldn't remember where he lived, but I knew it was far away. So really, I didn't know when I would ever see him again, but I wanted to. I ended up telling my best friend that I had met her friend's Uncle and that he was fine as hell! She told me that he was too old for me, but I assured her that I already knew that and we were just talking. Of course, she told me to be careful.

The next day came, and I couldn't wait to get home from school. I went over to my friend's house alone, because my best friend had to go to work after school. I went inside to see my friend, but was greeted by her uncle. He told me that his niece would be home soon and that I should wait... so I did. Before she came home, he called me upstairs to a bedroom. I went upstairs and we started talking. He instructed me to sit on the bed... so I did. Then, he asked to kiss me because my lips looked so soft. I couldn't resist him, so we kissed. Then, he pulled me on top of him. I wasn't comfortable up there, but didn't want to seem too immature, so I stayed. Eventually, he unlatched my bra.

"What are you doing?" I asked, surprised that he would go that far.

"Relax," he whispered as he held me tighter. "You better stop!"

I was so nervous and kept trying to pull away. " This is someone's room, and I don't want to get busted."

"Fine. Ok. Are you a virgin?" he asked.

"No."

"Are you sure?"

"I said no," I said with a slight attitude.

I don't know why I lied. I guess I didn't want to look inexperienced. *Why was it so hard for me to say the truth?* Maybe he wouldn't have continued making advances had I been honest. Shortly after, we heard my friend at the door. So, I snapped my bra back in place and left. He walked me downstairs. I remember my friend asked me what was going on.

We both nervously smiled and said, almost in unison, "Nothing."

"Ugh. Leave her alone!" She yelled at him.

"I'm not even bothering her! I was just about to walk her home."

He ended up walking me halfway home.

" Am I going to see you tomorrow? Just one last time?"

I knew he was about to head back home, so I told him I would.

The following day came, and as I was in school, I contemplated what was going to happen. I was amused that an older man *actually* wanted me. For some reason, it made me feel like a woman, and I enjoyed the attention. *Who needed a little boy, anyway? I was a young lady.* However, I was not ready for what happened next.

I thought I would kiss him and then see him off at the most. I also wanted to keep in touch for the next time he came to visit. I fantasized the entire day at school about this man. It was more so the vision of his face. I even thought to myself, I didn't even have my father around or my brothers to butt into my business.

I am grown now, and I can make my own decisions.

A part of me felt stripped.

I felt barren.

I felt naked.

I understood it was because I had no real accountability. As long as I wasn't in any kind of trouble, I didn't have to worry about anyone up my ass.

Up until this point, I had never been with a man. Just the thought of looking at this man and kissing him already made me nervous, but I did not consider sex as an option. I had restrained myself from being with anyone. My friends had been sexually active since the ages of 11 and 12...some were even younger. All I ever heard were their stories. However, it was never enough to make me want to do it, especially the stories about how painful it was and how you bled the first time. Trust me, a tampon up my cooch was enough. I was not looking forward to anything pertaining to sex.

After school came, I rushed home, called my friend, and asked her when she was going to be home. She told me she had to work and that I could come over after she got home. The hour got later and later. Then, he called. I was too nervous to answer. I took a deep breath when he hung up, but then he called back. I answered.

"When are you coming over? You can come now. You don't have to wait until she gets home."

I agreed and hung up the phone.

I guess I didn't come fast enough because he called again. He told me that he was leaving earlier than expected and that I needed to come say goodbye. So, I rushed down the street. It was almost dark when I left. When I rang the doorbell, he opened the door almost immediately. Then, we began to talk. It was nothing more than small talk.

"Why are you leaving a few days earlier?" I asked, confused.

"I found a ride willing to take me back so I have to go."

Then, he pulled me into the living room. I proceeded to look at the pictures on the shelves. There were pictures of this beautiful light-skinned baby.

"Who is this? She is beautiful." I asked, referring to the little baby girl.

"That's my new baby girl," he said to me.

"You just had a baby!?"

"Yes, but I'm not with the mother anymore."

"Oh ok." I replied just like some stupid naive little girl.

I was confused as to why he was so focused on me, especially after he just had a fresh, new baby.

"Man, I'm gonna miss you."

"I'm gonna miss you too!" I replied.

"Cool. I want to spend time with you before I go." I asked him when my friend was coming home. "She will be in soon."

"Cool," I replied shyly.

"Are you afraid of me?"

"No!"

Then, he leaned in and started kissing me as he guided my body to a thin blanket he had laid out on the carpet.

"You really know how to kiss, I see." I nodded my head. "Are you sure you are not a virgin."

I told him the same thing I told him the first time, "No."

He pulled off my pants. "Wait." I murmured. He ignored my comment.

Then, he pulled my panties off and told me to relax.

"I can't do it. I don't want to get pregnant."

He smirked. "Don't worry, you won't."

Then, I started to plead. " No! Please stop! I don't want to do this! Please stop!" I yelled.. "I haven't known you long enough for this. Please stop!"

"Stay still. It's ok. Just wait a minute."

Then, he pinned both of my wrists down, and with his knees, he pressed on my inner thighs to pry them open.

He put it inside of me.

Finally, I released my hands and I moaned in pain. "Stop. Please. It's hurting me! STOP!!"

As he continued to have sex with me, he moaned, "Wait a minute."

"Please, don't get me pregnant," I yelled as tears ran down my face.

He pulled out and ejaculated onto the carpet. I tried to jump up, but he forced me to hold still. Then, he got up, got a paper towel, and wiped this white substance off of me.

Finally, he released me.

As I was putting my clothes back on, he asked, "Why didn't you tell me you were a virgin?"

"Because I'm not a virgin."

" I can't tell. You must have been messing with some small niggas." He laughed.

"I just haven't done it in a long time."

He hugged me as if to ease over what he had just done.

"I'm going home now!"

"You not gone wait for your friend?"

"It's getting late. Just tell her to call me."

"Are you ok?"

"Yeah," I replied. I just wanted to leave.

He ended up walking me down the street, gave me a kiss, and told me that he loved me. I responded with the same. Again, I didn't understand why he said that. I just responded the same out of nervousness. He told me he would call me before he left. However, the next day, I heard he left, and he definitely didn't call me. I went into the house and briefly told my best friend that he had kissed me. She was against it because of his age, and she knew he was taking advantage of me. Because of this, I decided not to finish telling her what happened to me. I decided to take a bath, and I rocked myself to sleep.

I woke up screaming, having had a terrible dream. I actually experienced one of the worst nightmares of my life! I do not want to make up what I dreamt because it was so traumatic that I do not remember it entirely. I do remember being in a dark, smelly place. I was screaming because I felt all alone in this dark place. I remember calling out for my mother and father, but no one came. I continued trying to find my way in the dark place, but I could not see. I felt the presence of pure evil, and I actually felt the absence of love. I continued to scream! I remember thinking the name Jesus, but it wouldn't come out of my mouth. I was physically sweating and moaning on the bed. I started to feel fire burn up my legs. Then, my entire body was consumed with it.

I remember screaming.

"HELP ME! HELP ME PLEASE!"

After feeling exhausted and defeated for a while with no one to help me as I was burning, I felt myself slipping. I screamed out again as I was rocking in the bed.

"JESUS, HELP ME! HELP ME!"

I woke up to my best friend waking me up and telling me I was calling on Jesus to help me. I remember being soaking wet.

"What happened? she asked.

"I had a terrible nightmare of me burning in, what I perceived to be, HELL, but no one could help me." I trembled with great fear.

In the days to come, I was very ill. I refused to eat and had feelings of shame and guilt. I felt like my innocence was taken away from me because I had never experienced anything remotely close to this feeling. I was away from any feelings of love. I felt only emptiness, darkness, nakedness, guilt, shame, abandonment, judgment, condemnation, loneliness, and *hate*! I felt totally and completely void of feeling the love of God! This was the worst feeling ever! To not feel that God is with me has got to be the most horrible feeling I have ever felt in this lifetime!

I did not understand what was happening to me by sleeping with this stranger. All the people he had been with were now inside my body. It was too much to bear, and I could not handle it! I was already petite in size. Soaking wet, I had to be no more than 110 pounds. After two weeks of grieving because it felt like my soul was decaying, I couldn't eat much. My weight ended up being around 95 pounds.

My mother's friend noticed and wanted to have a talk with me one day. I told her I knew I was going through a spiritual attack and I needed to be saved. She helped me to repent so that I could receive the forgiveness of the Lord. I cried out to the Lord to save me again and deliver me. Shortly after, I began to feel homesick. I reached out to my mother and let her know I needed to come back home. I let her know I had been sick, and I couldn't take it anymore. Deep down, I needed the care of my mother. Two weeks later, I went back to New Jersey. I was greeted by my mother and father. My father gave me a sideways hug and said it was good to see me. I was overjoyed to be back because I had gained a different appreciation for my family.

I knew my life would never be the same again.

I did change. I felt renewed as far as my outlook on life. I had escaped to a place of no boundaries and barriers and went back to a place of limitations. This was a good thing for me. It was good because I didn't have so much freedom, I had both parents, and a home full of siblings. I couldn't come and go when I pleased. I had responsibilities, accountabilities, and I was checked on frequently. There was never an opportunity for me not to be accounted for. My whereabouts were always known because I had to come straight home after school. I had to do my chores, do my homework, and had to come inside before the streetlights came on. I also had to let my mother know what time I came inside just in case she fell asleep. When I went with friends, I had to tell my mother exactly who I was with.

I hated how my brothers could do things on their own without being checked on, but as for me, the rules were different. I was told because they were boys and knew how to take care of themselves, it was just different. Boys are stronger and can defend themselves. People take advantage of girls. Whatever! I was sick of it. Although I was able to go out sometimes and catch the bus to certain destinations, I always had to be accountable. Granted, I wasn't an adult yet; however, I was coming into my own and needed more space to figure that out – more space than I was given.

I couldn't tell you if our relationship got better ... it was just there. There was nothing to it. He didn't speak much to me. Hell, he may have even spoken less to me than when I left the first time. It was very eerie. I would look to him for approval and for any type of validation, but I received none. Once again, I was in this dry place with him and felt like a stranger in my own home. He would still give me rides to school, though. When he would give me a few dollars for snacks, he also gave me bananas. Til this day, I eat bananas because of him. I would tell him thank you for the treats, and he never responded verbally. He would just nod his head.

Days turned into months of this. I found out my father was no longer working his job because he was too sick. He must have been on disability or something because I remember how he took a paper route job. I know it sounds strange for a grown man to have such a job, but my mother said he just needed to do something to keep busy. He also wanted to contribute, seeing as though my mother was the breadwinner now.

My father did not like it when we said that because he felt that we disrespected him in our attitudes, as if he weren't the man of the house anymore. Who knows, maybe we did make him feel that way. All I knew was that my dad was always around now, and I did not like that. He was always lurking around and trying to catch me doing something wrong.

One day, I was watching tv when he came into the room, snatched the remote out of my hand, and told me to leave. No other words were spoken. I told him I was watching the TV, but he pushed me off the bed. At that point, my heart was raw and open. I was so tired of my father's bipolar attitude, and I didn't understand why he didn't just use his words to communicate to me how he felt. I would have accepted everything he said because I was always looking for him to answer the mystery as to why he treated me like crap. *I was his second daughter. Was I really that terrible in his eyes?* I started to scream, hyperventilate, and cry.

My youngest brother came into the room and asked me why I was doing what I was doing. I tried my best to explain what my father had done to me. At the same time, my dad turned his back as if he didn't even see or hear me and my brother.

I screamed and asked my brother, "WHY IS DADDY SO EVVVIIILLL?! WHY IS HE NOT TALKING TO ME?!"

He just shook his head. He didn't know either. I remember just going to my room and crying.

My experiences with my father caused me to become beyond bitter. A rage grew inside of me, and I didn't know what to do with it. I started acting out of character. I hated the school I attended. I had worked hard academically all of my life, only to end up at my community high school, all because we couldn't afford the previous private school I attended. It had been late in the school year when I returned from North Carolina, so I was placed in that high school at the end of my 10th grade year. I just knew that the next school year, I was going back to private school. However, after the summer came and went, I had to go back to the school I detested. So, I decided to stop applying myself.

For the first time in my life, I received a D in several subjects. Even I could not believe it! I felt like the school I was in was for dummies. I was so sure I was going to get all A's without even trying. To my surprise, if you do not work, never apply yourself, sit in class looking cute, it won't cut it. I was embarrassed. I hated my entire life! I was so lost, I couldn't find my way. I started dating older boys, and sometimes even men. Funny enough, when I went out with them and they tried to have sex with me, I refused them. I would cut them off cold and would refuse to see them again. Of course, they would call me and try to see me again, but in my eyes, it was a turn-off. I would enjoy them up until the point of them trying to lie with me. Then, I moved on to the next one.

My brother's friends were always trying to kick it with me, and at this point, I decided to kick it back. One of my youngest brother's friends became my boyfriend. He tried to be with me for the longest. After I got with him and we hung out, I eventually broke up with him. I just wasn't feeling him anymore. He continued to lurk around, so we had some kind of cat-and-mouse situation going on. We would always end up kissing behind somebody's house, my hallway, and eventually, at another friend's house. I decided it was that time, and he was going to be *the one*.

I remember I was almost 17 years old. His kisses had so much passion that they would leave me in a trance. Now, I realize it was a serious feeling of lust. I would get so aroused between my legs when I was kissing him. He never tried to go any further than touching and squeezing the little booty I did have. As we know, months of this kind of heavy kissing would always lead to other things.

One night, we went to his older friend's house, and I knew what time it was. I was bolder in thought than in actual action. I reflected back on the first experience I had, which wasn't pleasant, and I wondered if it would feel the same, especially seeing as though it was almost two years before. It started with his friend leaving us alone in the living room. Again, this must be a theme for me. The living room must be the breakout room.

No one ever heard of a bedroom?

He proceeded to take my shirt and pants off. Then, he put his hands between my legs. I was soaked. I couldn't believe what was about to happen, and this time I wanted it. He pulled out a condom and put it on. Hunny! It hurt much more this time. Way more than the first time. I had to push him back. He constantly asked me if I was ok. I said yes, but asked him why it hurt so much. He told me it was because he was big. It was big, yet he was only about a year older than me, only slightly taller, and a little stocky.

Anyways, we continued on. I remember feeling like I was being ripped. The deeper he went in, the more I held onto his back. The more pain I was in, the more he stuck his tongue deep into my mouth. Finally, he came. His friend walked into the room and asked, "Ya'll done?"

I was so embarrassed. Clearly, they both had a talk about what was about to go down. I quickly got dressed. We all hung out for a little bit, then they took me home. I'm sure they dropped me off somewhere random on the block because everyone would have known.

At that time, I didn't know much about sex, much less that a woman could climax. It was a while before I entertained him again. I was running because I knew it was wrong. I also knew I couldn't tell anyone about it. I may have told one friend, but she was the coolest girl on the block, by far. So, she was sexually active far beyond my years. She was older than I, friendly with everyone, and all the men loved her. She had taken me to many parties. If her parents only knew. She was actually my first friend when I moved to the neighborhood. I really missed the fun times we had. Her porch became my favorite spot.

I was also running from him because I had friends who I knew liked him, even though I talked to him first and had a relationship with him. There was something about me then; if I knew someone liked the person that liked me, I would try to hook them up. Kind of stupid, but that was me.

I started sneaking him in through my window. It was his idea. I thought he was bold, or maybe he was stupid. He risked being caught by three brothers and my father – the things men do for sex.

The dumb things we, as women, do to feel loved.

It was so sneaky, and it was scary. I panicked, but not enough to open up that good ol' window first. This time it hurt, but it hurt so good. When he finished, he went back out of the window. I could not believe I got away with that. It was so dangerous, but I liked it. It was about another month before I pulled that off again. One day, my father decided to nail the windows shut. My father actually took real nails, a hammer, and sealed my windows clean shut. I tried to get inside when I would sneak out, but could not.

My father gave us a certain time to be in the house. Even if I was sitting on the porch, it wasn't good enough. I was literally on a friend's porch when my father locked the doors. There I was, unable to get into the house because we didn't have a key then. So, I begged my youngest brother to open up my window, and he did. Next thing I know, before I was deep into my sleep, my father came through my bedroom door like the police and asked me when I got in the house. I told him I was already inside before the streetlights came on. Then, he noticed the nails had been moved on my window.

"I better not ever catch you sneaking in! I already checked your room and you were not in here!!"

"I was!" I replied again, hoping he would stop questioning me.

That was the last time I snuck in the house through the window. That's also the reason why I stopped sneaking him in that way. I went to his house once, but his aunt came home, so we left without doing anything. Shortly afterwards, I saw him with someone who was supposed to be my friend. Next thing I knew, she was having his children. That's the end of that story. That was the last sexual experience I had until I was 19 years old. I had some boyfriends in high school, but it never led to sex. I was also involved with a young guy whom I deemed as my first real love when I was 14 years old. Those were the days when life was sweet and simple... at least when it came to boys.

CHAPTER SIX: FAREWELL

My father had been in and out of the hospital a few times. I even visited him, but I didn't say much. Although my father was weak, thin, fragile, and sick, I still feared him very much, and it mattered to me what he thought of me. This particular time was scary. It didn't seem like he was going to make it, but he came home and lasted a few more months.

Remember, even when my dad was drunk, he was fun to be around. By now, he had stopped drinking for a couple of years; however, he continued smoking those stinking cigarettes. He only smoked them in his car or on the front porch. He never did it inside the house, though. During this time, he was still very mean and bitter. He didn't have the energy to actually beat us anymore, but he was very nonchalant and cold.

It was best if you didn't ask him anything because you would not get any information out of him. Honestly, I think he knew it was the end for him, and I can't imagine that feeling. The feeling of knowing that any day you will be forever separated from your wife and children. My middle brother was already away from us at school, and the rest of us definitely didn't spend any extra time with him...except for visiting him at the hospital. If anything, we all hated being home.

My father would call me so many inappropriate names that it wasn't even funny. It affected me so deeply that I tried to end my life because of how he made me feel – twice. The attempts I made to escape the pain were endless. As an adult, my mother reminded me that when my father would talk to me really rudely and nastily that it would tear me to shreds inside.

Yes, looking at it now, it seems foolish to allow any person, especially a man, to have this much control and power over my own will to live.

This was my father.

The first man I ever loved and looked up to was literally peeling my soul out from under me. Either he was teaching me to hate men, or to definitely become the strongest lesbian who ever lived. This male relationship would eventually shake my views on life and my perception of men to come. Needless to say, I made another attempt, which was actually my very first *real* attempt before the pills.

My father had talked to me roughly after I asked him something. Then, he acted as if he didn't know me. He acted as if it wasn't his responsibility to provide for me, feed me, or help me figure anything out. Growing up, there were commercials telling us to speak up and tell our parents that they are wrong...

Pure bullshit!

They CLEARLY didn't go home with those kids. They didn't know the mindsets of our crazy ass parents. Mess around and come to school with swollen ribs and injuries that the teachers can't see. Ask me how I know...

I must have been feeling brave one day, because I knew that anytime I had the nerve to go back and forth with my father in an attempt to understand was dangerous. I also knew I couldn't run away because I had already tried that. My oldest brother, with his long, skinny ass, road runner speed legs came busting around the corner to collect what was left of my *pathetic* self trying to run away. I only made it halfway down the block, only for him to carry me back to the house to receive a huge spanking.

It's always your own blood who turns against you!!

To continue, I just tried to end it all. My thoughts were, *I will fix him once and for all. I will make him hurt just as much, if not more, than he had hurt me. I will get a wire hanger, loop it around another hanger, throw it over the door, close it, put my head through the hanger, and hang myself until I can't breathe.*

Clearly, I hadn't thought this plan through. I must have been winging this. I was very small, always petite. I couldn't have been more than 75-80 pounds, and that's a stretch. To my surprise, my mother walked in and saw... or should I say caught... the pure foolishness of a hurt child.

She said, "Aww Angie, no! I'm so sorry for what your father said to you!"

She helped me get out of that entanglement and held me as I cried.

I wanted to die!

I really wanted the pain to end. I vowed never to let a man have that much power over my emotions, never. My mother would always say to me, "Your dad is going to affect the way you see men. I wonder how your relationships with men will be in the future."

One thing was always true. I never trusted men, and I never will 'til this day.

Now that my father is this man whom I no longer respect because he's in a vulnerable state, I started to not take him seriously. Don't get me wrong, I obeyed him...I always had. I just looked at him with such disgust, I was rebellious in my soul, and I questioned everything.

As I got older, my relationship with my father grew more and more confusing. Sometimes he would speak; at most times, he wouldn't. I did not or could not figure out what the secret was to get him to talk. *Was it something I did or didn't do to encourage his behavior?* I looked for signs and entryways to even approach him, but this man was absolutely impossible. It was better if I just stayed out of his way. So, I decided to start studying the scriptures and find out about this love that God had for me, which obviously allowed this cruel treatment of me. I could not understand, if this God loved me so much, why wasn't he helping me? I couldn't understand why he would put me in this family to start. It was all so confusing to me, and I needed to understand. I needed to find a way to be able to digest what was happening in my life.

My mother was so in love with the Lord that all she talked about was Jesus. She would tell us to read and become saved, for real. For all we knew, we were saved, but I knew I was not free. I was trapped in this small body, and I felt nothing but pain. I was so insecure with how I looked physically, and now my emotions matched how I felt on the outside. My father did not acknowledge any of my efforts, my academics, or my being a good child. He left me so open for men to come in and fill my head with nothing but lies, so much so that when men approached me, I pushed them away. I didn't believe one positive thing they said. I felt everything they would say to me was a complete lie. I believed that all they wanted was sex. Most times, I was right, but not all the time. Some men were sweet, but sweet didn't make me happy, though. I needed someone strong, but I knew I didn't want a man who hit me.

Oh, HELL NO!

If he wasn't aggressive and outspoken, and manly or controlling, I wanted nothing to do with him. I hated weak men. It was the biggest turn-off... and PLEASE don't be a crying man! That was a complete deal breaker for me. *Who was dealing with an emotional man who cries just to express his love for me?* I didn't have time for that. Besides, that was something I never saw, not even from my dying father.

I began to seek the Lord, and I started praying. Finally, I felt the presence of the lord, and I began to dance for the Lord. He had given me a gift, and he only knew how to interpret the meanings of my every move. I began to express the pain and the hurt through this gift he had given me, and I was blessed to have a church that accepted the gift of dance. My heart grew softer.

One day, I went to a special service at a church in Newark. There was a popular preacher there the night I was invited. He called me out of the many people and cast out the spirit of unforgiveness that had lived and grown inside me.

I was angry!

Without touching me, right from my seat, I was on fire. I felt the Holy Spirit burn the evil that lay inside of me. I began to scream and shout. For the first time, I caught the Holy Ghost...*black folks say that when we dance for the Lord.* It was like fire caught up in my bones, and I was wild! After it was over, I cried profusely. I remember feeling a huge relief.

I felt free.

I wasn't angry.

I wasn't trapped.

I felt like I could breathe.

I felt like I could see clearly, and I had just experienced what it felt like to be delivered by God! I was grateful beyond measure.

That night, I went home and noticed that my heart grew kinder towards my father. I'm glad it did because the 23rd of April was my birthday. That day, I was commissioned by a mother of the church. Her name was Mother Theresa. She told me I needed to see my father that day. We were at a second service in church, and I had already seen my dad a couple of days before that. He had been admitted to the hospital again for about a week. This time, they put a stint inside of him, and he stopped talking altogether. We just knew he was coming home like all the other times. My father was the strongest man we knew. He was always that strongman who worked at Conrail Railroads. He was always the man who commanded our attention... the man whom I have never seen anyone disrespect.

So, why was this time any different than all the times he would get sick and come home? Mother Teresa instructed me to go to his hospital bedside and tell him how I felt. She told me that I had to forgive him. She also told me to ask him to forgive me. She said I needed to be forgiven for the way I treated him. Had I not been seeking the Lord at that time, I would have never received what she said.

Old Angie would have felt justified because of the hurt and pain my father had caused me. *Why should I apologize to him?* I understand now. When you're in Christ, the word of God shows you who you really are. He shows us that we are all filthy rags in need of a savior. He showed me that he was the judge of us all, and that I had no right to cast judgment on my father. If I didn't forgive my father, then he couldn't go against his own word and forgive me. I was smart enough to know that I needed the forgiveness of the Lord just to live.

With that being said, I ran to my father's bedside on my birthday. I was so happy because I actually listened to Mother Teresa. I walked into my father's room that evening before closing hours. I was surprised when I saw the oxygen mask on his face, and he wasn't talking or fully aware of his surroundings. My mother went beside him on the left side of the bed, bent over, and gave his head a kiss. I went over and did the same.

Then, I said, "Hi, Daddy. It's Angie."

He opened his eyes slightly. My mom asked me if I wanted to talk to him, and I said that I did. She asked me if I needed her to stay.

"I need to do this alone," I replied.

She gave me a kiss and walked out of the room. I turned to my father and sat down beside him. Then, I began to talk about the things that were happening at home. I told him that I was instructed to say some things, and I decided to talk straight from the heart. I was so brave, yet so nervous at the same time. The fact that I was bold enough to express the hurt and pain he caused me, without falling out on the floor from fear, was amazing. Then, I took his hand and I told him that he is free to go to Heaven. I assured him that we would be ok, and I told him that I didn't want him to be in any pain. The most important thing I did was ask him to forgive me. I acknowledged my part in disrespecting him and rebelling against him.

A tear ran down my father's face. He put his hand on his mask in an attempt to pull it off. I quickly reacted to him and said, "Daddy, you have to keep your mask on."

I put the mask back on him. He made three attempts before he gave up. I wiped the tears from his face. I could not believe what I was witnessing. In all of my seventeen years of life, I never saw my father cry. Honestly, I didn't think he could. He always appeared as a hard, strict, and cold man. To my amazement, he could. He wasn't the huge monster I made up in my heart. He was an actual human being, and he was hurt. He *actually* had feelings. His heart was in complete pain, just as mine was. It was just for different reasons, and he was dying. I freed us both. My mother and I went home. We didn't say much to each other, but she said she was proud of me. That was how I spent my birthday. I woke up the next day to get ready for school, and I felt lighter. I was anxious because I was waiting for the phone call that my dad didn't make it through the night.

I was pretty quiet while at school, and to my surprise, my mother picked me up from school. She dropped me off at home and told me she was going to see my dad. She said she needed to see him as much as she could while she still could. She asked me if I wanted to join her. I let her know that I saw him enough, I was ok, and that I understood her need to be with him.

I grew tired the very next hour and decided to take a nap in my mother and father's bed. I felt different. I felt like I knew something was about to happen. *Why else would the church mother tell me to see him the day before?* I was prepared. I already knew. I fell into a deep sleep and had a dream.

In the dream, I was with my father. He was taking me walking in the area where we used to live in the past. I was a little girl again.

I asked my father, "Hey, Daddy. What did you teach me?"

He told me that he taught me a lot. However, his words became mute. I heard nothing. Then, he took my hand as we crossed the street. He put me on the left side of him and told me that little girls are to walk on the inside of the sidewalk, leaving the man closer to the street. In case anything happened, he would be able to push me further on the ground and closer to the stores. Then, whatever danger happened, it would get him and not me. This actual conversation was more than a dream because I was actually 4 or 5 years old when he told me that. I was actually dreaming of a real memory. A memory I had long forgotten. He then took my right hand, and we walked into the sunset. I felt more protected in that one instance than I have ever felt with any man in my entire life. A child's innocence, placing complete trust in her father, feels like floating on a cloud in the sky. There is a quiet assurance that she will not fall through.

I woke up to the sound of my mother entering the house. The front door was through her bedroom. I sat up in bed. My mother walked in slowly and began to speak almost in a whisper.

I looked at her and said, "Mommy, I already know. He walked me down the street into the sunset, holding my hand. So, I know he's gone."

"Yes he is. Where are your brothers and sister?"

We all met my mother in the living room, which was the next room over. The only thing separating the rooms was a big curtain. As my mother broke the news to us, we all just looked at each other.

None of us cried.

We really didn't know how to respond. I don't think we thought that day would ever come. We felt like he was too strong, and could actually defeat death itself. So, we continued to look at each other.

My youngest brother slapped himself against the head and said, "What is wrong with me? I can't even make myself cry!"

I went back into Mom's bedroom, sat on the bed, and pondered how I was able to see him in my dream moments before or even after he had already passed. I began to question my mother about the time he passed, and found out I was dreaming at that time. The dream ended when Mom arrived home.

I told myself at the funeral that I would not cry at all. I told myself I had to be strong for my mother and that I needed to be strong for my family and friends. His children didn't need to break down. We all needed to remain solid, and that's what we all did. I don't recall if my sister cried or not. I do know my brothers did not cry and neither did I. Of course my mother cried, but not nearly as badly as my father's siblings. I had cousins who could barely handle it, but his children didn't do an outward display of grief. There was enough time to do that later. My sister and I wore white. We wanted to demonstrate my father's new life. Meanwhile, everyone else wore black.

If anyone knew what my father really died from, they didn't say anything to me. They dared not tell me about a rumor they heard. As far as his family, we kept it on a hush. I don't recall ever having a conversation about what we would say if people asked us. I think it was common sense to just lie. Some things don't need to be said. When close friends asked me, I told them he died because of his lungs and smoking too much. Having AIDS back then was shameful. It was a germ. It was the most misunderstood and feared disease of that time.

The things ignorance will do to a nation, and that same corruption starts within the family. If I could change anything that happened to my father, it would be to prevent him from ever going to Vietnam. Yes, I could just take away his disease. However, according to my mother, friends, and family, the terrors of that war is what killed him. He came back a changed man. He was no longer the missionary who got deported. My father's entire life was different. My mother deserved the man who left, not the one who walked in years later. She deserved someone who wasn't an alcoholic, an abuser, or an emotionally disconnected man. My mother always says she has "E.L.M. SEEDS," Erving Lee Mitchell's seeds.

That was her joy.

I never knew the man that she once knew and had a healthy relationship with. As his children, we were all cheated. We were dysfunctional. *Was my father a victim of his circumstances? Or was he just a cheater who had issues and turned to alcohol?*

At the end of the day, none of that matters because what happened... happened. It was too late. We don't have the power to reverse time.

Would we really ever learn if we could erase our mistakes? How could we take responsibility for our behaviors? How would we learn and become better people?

Unfortunately, some of us never learn from our mistakes and bad choices. Some people die in their sins. I'm grateful my father knew God, and I pray the Lord received him with open arms. I'm glad my father turned from his evil ways and accepted God's forgiveness. My mother says 'til this day that my father was a good man.

Does being a good man make them a good father?

My father did what he knew to do. That is something I have had to accept in order to move forward. I could no longer blame my father for being miserable. Everything I did from that day forward, was totally my responsibility.

Who was going to accept the reasons why I had anger issues? Who was going to care to hear the reasons why I didn't want to commit to anyone? Who was gonna hear how I really felt?

I hated men while still trying to outwardly love them. I would learn for the next 30-plus years that I couldn't run away from everything. Some things had to be dealt with. I needed healing from a lot of hurt and rejection from men in general. My relationship was broken, and partly because I was broken.

Why was I attracting these toxic ass men? Did I have a huge badge on me that read, 'VULNERABLE WOMAN LOOKING TO BE ABUSED?'... and so, my journey began.

CHAPTER SEVEN: THIS AIN'T LOVE

Let's start this voyage by dating a drug dealer with two children. He was a known fighter, troublemaker...basically any and all things related. Oh, and I forgot to mention he was also a friend of my oldest brother. They knew each other from school and the block, but they didn't hang out. My brother never warned me about his reputation, but when he found out we were dating, he just told me that I would see what they were saying. I asked him questions and he just ignored them. He only told me that he was not going to tell me what to do because I'm grown.

"You're just gonna do what you want anyway", my brother said to me.

That was the type of person I was. I loved challenges, and I was extremely competitive, so that comment only made me want his friend more. Besides, I liked bad boys at that time. I didn't want someone straight out of jail or anything. I just wanted someone with muscles, a good job, respectful, and who was cute. He supposedly had a steady job, but the way he had my wrist lit with gold, the breakfast and dinner dates, and going shopping, I knew for sure the money did not come from his job. Only thing was, he was a total control freak. At first, I loved the attention, but I would soon experience what his anger felt like when I accused him of cheating. I would end up pinned against his wall, struggling to breathe. Let's just talk about the beginning.

I was the type of girl who was hard to get, especially if I liked you. They called me both sweet and spicy when it came to my personality. I wasn't the shy type. However, I was kind of private, and I didn't like too much attention. I was very outspoken, and I enjoyed a guy who was just as intelligent as I was. I had always been the type to ask mind questions. You know, those deep questions that would leave some people speechless. It was a joy to see them sweat from not knowing how to deal with me. Only those who knew how to flow with me made me melt.

This man was about 5 years older than I, who was 19 years old at the time. This man picked me up from everywhere. He would not allow me to even go to college without dropping me off. I recall the first time I spent the night out with him. My mother told him to make sure he takes care of me. I was shocked! At that time, I was coming in the house very late. One day I said, "I'm just gonna stay at his apartment." That's when the intimacy grew.

He grew extremely possessive. He bought me a brown pager because brown is my favorite color. He wanted to keep a tight hold on me. When he paged me, I had to call back right away. The problem was, back then, I didn't own a cell phone. We took a few short trips together, but it seemed like we were *always* together. I felt like I needed a little space because things were going so fast.

Yes, he bought me things and treated me like a lady. My only complaint was his control. He was jealous when I went out with friends, and he began showing up at events I attended...it was *out of control*. He also had an ex-girlfriend who was trying to work her way back into his life. Did I mention he was friends with her *still?*

One day, she showed up at his home when we were in the room together. From that point on, I became suspicious. His older brother knocked on his bedroom door and told him that she wanted to talk to him, but he refused. His ex must have felt disrespected because the next thing we knew, she had slit his tires. He went outside and lost it! When he came back upstairs into the house, he was really upset. As soon as he walked into his bedroom, I began with my interrogation.

"WHY ARE YOU TALKING TO YOUR EX-GIRLFRIEND? I KNEW YOU TWO HAD SOMETHING GOING ON!!" I yelled.

He continued to deny it and tried to make me believe that she talks to his mother sometimes, but nothing was going on. Of course, I did not believe a word he said.

"Take me home now!"

At the same time, his brother was knocking on the door, whispering to him to keep it down because of the police. He opened up the door and told him that he didn't give a fuck. He closed the door and continued to defend himself. To no avail, I headed for the door, grabbed my beeper, and tried to leave the room. This man took my beeper, slammed it on the floor, and told me to sit down.

Then, he said, "You ain't going nowhere! SIT YO'ASS DOWN!"

He left the room because he heard the girl come up the stairs again. His brother convinced her to leave, but not before he threatened her. When my boyfriend came back into the room, I tried to slide out through the crack of the door. He grabbed me and threw me against the bed. I got up and started to throw punches at his face, but he was much taller than I. Sadly, my sorry attempts at punching him failed. He took both of my wrists, twisted them above my head, and pinned me against the wall, but I got away from him. I began to scratch him. In two seconds, from that moment, my neck was in both of his hands, my legs were dangling from under me, and my shoulders felt like they were being disconnected from my body.

Did I also mention that I could hardly breathe? I stopped hitting him because I was busy gasping for air. He dropped me! I fell to the floor like dead weight. My neck was burning! This man actually tried to choke me out. As I peeled myself off the floor, all I could say was, "You just wait till I tell my mother!"

When he told me that he didn't care, I was in awe! Before that swing of violence, he did respect my mother.

I yelled out, "I HATE YOU! You just wait till I tell my brothers!" Thing is, I knew that I wasn't going to tell them at all, because I wouldn't want my family to be involved in more drama. This drama was street stuff involving outsiders. That war would have led to someone dying. It wasn't worth all of that.

I decided not to tell them anytime soon. I decided to count my losses and leave out alive and well. His response was that he would kill my entire family. I just pleaded for him to take me home. His brother came into the room and gave him his BMW keys. He told him to just take me home. So, we walked to the car, and he proceeded to take me home. I asked him why he was driving so slowly. He said he wanted to talk to me.

Of course, he continues to tell me how he does so much for me...blah, blah, blah. I wasn't hearing anything he was saying. He sounded like a whiny little boy who was crying to his momma. I was busy rubbing my sore neck. I had his fingerprints embedded, and it hurt just to turn my neck. Come to think about it, my entire body was sore. I remember the middle of my back throbbing. I could not believe what had happened to me. I actually thought he loved me too much to put his hands on me. If control was love, then I guess he did love me.

He was actually kind of obsessed with me. I didn't realize it was his control at first. I thought that it was because he was my first adult boyfriend, and the things he did only went with the territory. Men do things for women and protect them. Women listen, do what the man says, and give them continual sex. My problem was both. I didn't enjoy sex the way I should have at that age. I really didn't learn about pleasing a man until much later. Any sexual experience I had before then was me lying there. I wasn't a participant.

Also, I didn't listen too much. I was very combative. I needed a challenge. I would say that I needed to be strong with my lady views. So, I didn't understand that this man wanted it his way, and as long as he controlled things, I couldn't make decisions. Here we have another problem, because there was no way I was going to allow my boyfriend to tell me what to do on a regular basis.

What's the point of having my own mind?

I had been told what to do by a lot of people, my entire life. I was over it! So, once again, I rebelled because I was being restrained. This man had the audacity to pull over at the park in an attempt to talk to me.

I yelled. "WHAT ARE YOU DOING? DONT STOP. TAKE ME HOME NOW!!"

He said he would, but only after he talked to me. I listened to him blame me for everything. He said he would deal with his ex-girlfriend, but as for me, he continued to defend his honor.

Eventually, I said," Ok, please take me home. My neck hurts badly. We can talk later."

He made me promise that I would answer his calls. As soon as we pulled up to my house, I jumped out and screamed, "I never want to see you again! It's over!"

For days, I was stalked by him, trying to talk to me, or pulling up to my house. Eventually, it stopped, but this time he was angry. He told me that he would blow up my house with us inside if I did not give him the jewelry he bought me.

So, you understand now? As long as I stayed with him, those things were mine. I guess I was only borrowing them. He could control me as long as he did things for me. I did not like that one bit. Gifts are meant to stay with the recipient of the item. Men can't have their way with women, so they take back those cherished things the woman desired.

What did he think? I was really going to ignore my sore and swollen neck. Was I really going to continue dating him on the strength of keeping some jewels?

Man please! Wrong girl. Wrong day. It was my specialty to dismiss and ignore men. He would soon find out that he was already forgotten!

One day, he told me that he would blow up my house and even fight my brothers if I didn't give him his stuff back. I decided not to cause any more attention to my situation and become more of an embarrassment, so I packed up his stuff and returned it.

All he said was, "You think Imma let you wear my stuff with another man?"

I said, " Ok then, Goodbye. You thought I was gonna keep this stuff so you can keep coming here? Take it! I don't care!"

I closed my door and was finally relieved. I didn't see him for a while. Life continued. I was dating people in my school, and I saw him with a woman in a red car on a random day.

One time, he came to my side door to ask me to go out with him. I told him that I saw him in the red car. He told me that the girl liked him, and she was nice.

"I guess so if you're driving her car," I said.

Months later, he was about to marry her... so I heard. I entertained a few relationships afterwards. Not one of them lasted past 6 months because their personalities ran stale to me. They started to get boring. Everything could be good, but then they would either say something stupid or they wouldn't keep their word about something. That was also huge to me. If I found out you lied, that would be grounds for dismissal. I didn't have any room for grace. Let God be the only one giving out grace because I was two lifetimes short of giving out grace.

Then, all of a sudden, they started to not be as attractive as when we first hooked up. I liked men who made me laugh and men who had ambition. I did not want to be involved with someone who had no plan in life. Another thing, they seemed to fall for me quickly, and that was a turn-off to me. Then you run into the liar. They were the ones who just made up full stories as soon as you met them. They are the ones you give your phone number to in hopes that all the bragging about themselves was true.

How come when it's time for us to go on a date, that Lexus Coupe you had all of a sudden goes to the shop, or better yet, your momma had to borrow it? All they really did was fabricate their lives in hopes of some premature pussy. I'm far from a gold digger. All I cared about was their words being true. I would literally watch their lies unfold before my eyes. Next thing I knew, I was telling them I could no longer be with them, or I would just disappear.

I was now 21 years old and already tired of the bull crap. All men seemed to be the same. The biggest con artist would soon change my entire life more so than anyone else. Up until this day, I have him to thank. I had several relationships in between. However, this one cut the cake.

CHAPTER EIGHT: THE CONCEPTION STORY

I first saw him in the laundromat when I was 19 years old. We glanced at each other and gave each other the googly eyes. Nothing much was said, so I continued to do my laundry. Thank goodness because the last thing I needed was him coming over to talk to me, and end up seeing my underwear, especially the period panties! That would have been a huge error. Not to mention, I don't have good conversations while folding clothes. I wanted to be in and out. I quickly packed up my clothes, took one last glance at him, and went home.

It took me about seven minutes to get home. I definitely wondered about him later. He had curly hair and stood at about 6 feet tall. He had that texturizer in his hair because it didn't look like natural curls. He also always wore this red cap. I later learned that it was his signature look....Timberland boots and a red cap. He was medium brown skinned, a little darker-skinned than I was. He was cute or whatever, but he was thin. There was not an ounce of fat on those bones.

Next time I would see him was on the bus. I was coming back from somewhere and was on the back of the bus. Contrary to what our ancestors experienced on the bus and the rights that were fought for us, the young people of my time enjoyed the back of the bus. Most of the time, it was pure trouble to sit back there. I absolutely hated it.

This particular bus line was dirty and smelly. There were always drug needles, piss, used condom wrappers, beer cans, and cigarette butts left on the floor. It was gross! Honestly, I preferred the front, if I could help it. I was getting off at my stop, which was also his stop. We both walked off and, yet again, glanced at one another.

I said to him, "You're the guy from the laundromat."

He smiled and said, "Yes, and so are you."

Even though we were walking in the same direction, he walked much faster, and pretty soon, he was out of my view. About two weeks later, I was with my boyfriend... the same boyfriend who would later stalk me after his attempt to strangle me. Early on in our relationship, he introduced me to some of his friends. Funny thing, he was one of those friends I was later introduced to. His name won't be mentioned throughout this story.

Unfortunately, our meeting is relevant, but he is not.

We went on a couple of double dates when I was in that relationship. He appeared extremely clingy and needy when he dated those other girls. He was also very passionate. He liked to hold their hand and kiss them a lot. Actually, I wish that I had met him first. He was sweeter and more attractive than my boyfriend. My boyfriend was the more aggressive and controlling of the two.

One day, as his friend was walking down the street, I crossed over to get to my block, which he was on. He had just had a baby. I knew this because he took a picture of his child out of his back pocket and showed it to me. I congratulated him and told him that his baby was beautiful. He was a handsome, light-skinned baby boy. He couldn't have been any more than one month old. He told me that the mother had moved to another city, so I assumed they were not together anymore. On all the double dates we went on, none of those girls were the mother.

As I walked away, I remember wondering about how our baby would look, because he sure made a gorgeous baby. One thing I noticed when we all went out together, I started to feel like he was jealous of my boyfriend. My boyfriend would always buy me anything, and always took me out. Later, I found out that he flipped the bill the majority of the time for his friend.

Anyways, he lusted after my boyfriend's things, including wishing he had me. In a way, I wanted his passion. So, the way we looked at each other changed. Whenever my boyfriend and I broke up, he would send his friend to talk to me. Because of his friend's sweet and persuasive ways, I would constantly take my boyfriend back. When my boyfriend and I finally broke up for good, his friend hadn't been around. Then, he magically showed up.

At that time, I also had a friend who needed a place to stay until she got an apartment. I guess she stayed for a couple of weeks. I ended up hooking those two up, and they continued having a sexual relationship. When she moved, she got back with her children's father from high school. Shortly after that, my family moved across town.

One day, out of the blue, I saw him in my new neighborhood. He was staying with his great aunt. He would walk about ten minutes to see me at my apartment. At first, he was allowed inside. We were friends after all. Plus, he no longer saw or hung out with my ex, so we never crossed the line until he asked me out. We would go out and hang with some of my friends, and we would go to the movies. I don't recall us ever going out to eat.

One day, while I was at work, my ex came up to my job and called himself telling me off because he found out I was dating his friend. I was the one who told my girlfriend that, if she ever saw him again, tell him that I had found someone better than him and that I didn't care about him anymore anyway. That particular message was well received because he was in my face. He wished me well.

His actual words were, "You went from a steak to a hamburger, so you downgraded."

As he laughed, he then told me that he was on his way to kick his friend's ass, and the only thing that saved him was his older brother. He said that he wasn't worth it. I told him that they weren't even friends anymore, and whoever I was dating was none of his business. At the time, it felt like a game. I was happy that he was upset, only because I was not intimate with him, and didn't really want a relationship with his friend. He was weak in my eyes. He was also a whore. Crazy thing is, I already knew that.

We would have conversations about the future, but his goals were all over the place. It seemed as though he didn't know what he wanted. All he wanted to do was kiss... and kiss some more. Then, he invited me over to his great aunt's apartment. They lived in this building in the neighborhood. I went there twice to see him, but I was so uncomfortable because there were so many people living there. There was no real privacy. He tried to convince me to have oral sex with him there, and I wasn't the one who was going to perform. I allowed him to touch me, but it ended there. Then, I asked him to walk me home. When we arrived at my apartment, he gave me a heavy kiss goodbye. I remember this car riding by us, and this girl yelled out, "Don't do it, girl. He be with everybody! Don't do it!" Since she was laughing, I didn't take her seriously. However, I did ask him who that was and what it was that she was talking about. He said that it was someone he didn't know who was trying to start trouble.

I wish with all my heart I had listened. I did try to stay away from him, but not before it was too late. My decision not to see him anymore without a reason wasn't good enough for him. He laid it on even stronger. He would ask to buy me things or give me money. One day, I finally asked for $40. I couldn't believe it when he gave it to me. I really didn't believe this man had two pots to piss in. He had a serious spirit of lust that would not stop pursuing me. He begged me to come outside to see him, and I did. He pushed me into the back hallway and tried to have sex with me.

I remember I said," HELL TO THE NO!! I'm not doing that here in this dirty hall. Are you crazy?"

He said, "Ok, but please let me taste it. Just sit back, it will be ok. Just a little. I want to make you feel good," he said.

So, I leaned back and let him perform oral sex on me. I moaned and groaned because it felt so amazing. I stopped him in the middle of it because I became afraid we would get caught. I was also afraid that if it didn't stop, then I would have let him have me all the way. We stopped, and I sat up to fix my clothes. He grabbed my hand and pressed it against his crotch. I was shocked at how big it felt because he was so thin and frail and didn't have any weight to him. I don't know. I just know I was like, "That thing ain't going into me." I pulled my hand away and went into the house.

Later, I told him that I couldn't see him anymore. I was not ready for a sexual relationship, and technically, we were not even a real couple. I was in college, and I didn't have time to get messed up behind some boy. Plus, I was in church. Yes, throughout all of this misbehaving, I was committed to church. I was one of the dance leaders, and here I was, living the good 'ole life of sin. Well, it really wasn't that good because I felt dirty and gross after I did anything sinful. I ended up repenting or risking becoming physically sick.

We will save that story for another chapter.

Anyway, I wasn't getting away with anything. I always paid for my sins one way or another. My life would soon show that you reap what you sow. It would show that the things I spoke about had a way of making it into reality, especially the bad. As ambitious a person I was, the devil equally tripped me up. Somehow, in the mix of things, God's grace still covered me. I was not consumed by evil. I still had a heart that wanted God. I just wish that I had a stronger will to keep his commandments more than I wanted the approval of man.

Since I can't go back and change my past, my hope is that you don't fall into the many traps that I could have avoided. I believe if you want to be kept, then you will. He will keep you. God will sustain you. However, he won't go against your own will. Remember, he fights for you, not with you. If you live a life of sin continually, eventually it will catch up with you, stop you in your tracks, and overtake you.

Eventually, I was overtaken by a spirit of lust. I remember the day it entered me. After that day, I had a strong desire to be with that man. Before that happened, I told him I would not see him anymore, and I didn't. I moved away and began my life in a different location that was back on the other side of town. I was finally free.

How many of you know that what you don't defeat, you are destined to repeat?

In some shape or form, it rears its ugly head back into your life. I was dancing in church, stronger than I had before. The saints were being blessed through that ministry of dance. Then, this clown started trying to pick me up from work. He started treating me even nicer. He wanted to go on walks through the park and all. I even went to a doctor's appointment with him. I don't even know where the car came from because he didn't have any money.

One day, he kissed me at the park under the park lights. I began to ask him about his life and talk about God, and he started to become childish. He spoke more softly and started to express how no one loves him in the right way. He talked about how every woman he was with wanted to leave him, including me. I tried to make him understand that I didn't want to live a life separated from God because of sin. I tried to explain that I couldn't be blessed fully living in sin.

After that, he told me that he loved me, but I told him that I couldn't have a relationship with him. He started to plead with me and asked me what was wrong with him. He told me he was an open book and would tell me whatever I wanted to know about him. According to him, he had no secrets. Up until that point, I didn't know a liar could be so cunning and believable. Next thing I knew, he grabbed me and kissed me passionately. I remember looking up into the light because it felt like something came out of me and entered my soul. I didn't know what it was.

Of course, being more mature in Christ, especially concerning the supernatural, I definitely understand now. It caused me to feel more lustful and made me fantasize about him and me. I was home burning between my legs. However, because of pride, I still refused to call him. Those demons study you, though. They know your every move. We fail to realize that these demonic entities are ancient. They have been here before man existed. The ones that fell from Heaven hate our Lord and savior Jesus Christ because God loves us, and the demons hate us even more. Their entire goal is to steal, kill, and destroy us. We will never reach the promised land. If it were up to them, we would remain in constant warfare with them.

With that being said, they must have whispered into his good left ear and told him I wanted him. He called me two weeks later and asked to see me one last time. He wanted to take me to the movies to see Mission Impossible 2. I agreed and went with him for the last time. On his way to drop me off at home, he decided to surprise me by taking me to the park. It was a park with a lake and boat rides. Problem was, it was 1 am.

Why are we at the park when it's completely empty? This wasn't going to be a smooth ride by far. "Angie, what have you gotten yourself into?"

The park was under construction because there were heaps of dirt everywhere. The beautiful park I once admired, with its lake and boats, was now incomplete. It wasn't romantic at all. *He clearly didn't know, or why else would he bring me here?* He told me that he wanted to come because, at night, it was serene and beautiful. *Who the hell was he kidding?* It was everything but that. Yes, we were alone, but I could have talked to him one last time outside my home. I damn sure didn't need to be there at 1 am.

"Why do you want to be here?" I asked.

He replied, "I just wanted to be alone with you. I didn't want the night to end."

He reached over and started to kiss me. It grew intense.

I got nervous and said, "Maybe you should take me home."

He continued to kiss me and asked if he could come over to my side.

I said, "Ok."

So, he crawled over to my side in the passenger seat. I was so uncomfortable, so he tilted my seat back. We continued kissing heavily. Then, he began to touch my private area. The more he touched it, the more it felt good – the more my conviction rose. Then, on the radio, a song came on. It was a song I had long loved with a deep melody. One of my favorite artists played.

Who would have known this song was prophetic?

Every word he sang…every word he spoke… was actually happening. My black pants leg came off. Just one leg was all that was needed. I don't want anyone to think I didn't *want* it. Even though it wasn't my plan, my mind said no, but my body said yes. I say that because I didn't refuse. I allowed this man to put his penis inside of me. I was soaked from the arousal, and the piece of him I admired before was now inside of me. In the background, Maxwell was playing. My favorite song played automatically on what may have been his playlist.

Did he know this was my song? Who could resist the sultry sound of Maxwell? A recipe for disaster was brewing. As he sang, "Pray God you can cope, I stand outside, this woman's work, this woman's work, oh it's hard on a man. Now his part is over, now starts the craft of the father."

This song would become my life. If I only knew!

So many things I wanted to say. I cared about this man. I just knew I didn't want to continue to live a life I knew displeased God. He was sneaky, and I could feel it in my soul! I just couldn't prove what I felt. We weren't talking marriage or anything, but he claimed to have wanted to be in a serious relationship with me. My gut told me that every word that came from this man's mouth was a lie. This man clearly lived in a fantasy. I should have known because nothing bothered him on the outside, and he was extremely calm…a little calm. He was also sweet and very affectionate. He wasn't in touch with reality. Everything was always so sensual and seductive, as if all life was about was passion and sex. He had some sick obsession. It was clearly something he was lacking in childhood, or maybe even the trauma he witnessed. I believe he was trying to make up for his hurt by being promiscuous.

Yes, my gut told me that there were a lot of us. If I only listened to that small voice. If I had stopped looking for some huge atom to fall out of the sky and land in my face in order for me to see the truth, my life would have gone differently.

This man was a womanizer in all forms! A legion of demons indeed, and that seducing demon did just that to me. It consumed me. It clouded my entire judgment. Strange enough, as he was pumping in and out of me, and the song played, the Lord gave me a vision of the future. One pump, I saw myself pregnant, two pumps, I saw him leave me, and the last and final pump, before I pulled his penis out of me with my hand, I saw that I had a baby girl. I was in shock! The song was telling the future, and even in my sin, God allowed me to see what was in store for me.

I was pregnant!

His part was to get me pregnant, with three pumps and no ejaculation, but pre cum. *How foolish was I to experience such a thing without the full effects of good sex?* Not only that, but I was guilt-ridden, and I was traumatized by my future. According to the song, his part was over, and now the craft of the father. Yes, this man's job was done before it even started. At the time I'm writing this book, my ***only*** daughter is 22 years old, and he has yet to see her face-to-face. I would say his job is definitely over.

Straight coward! I will talk about that later.

For now, I had a vision of being a single parent, without the physical knowledge that I was pregnant, but the spiritual understanding was surely there.

I panicked and started screaming, LOUDLY, "Oh my God, what did you do? What did you do? Get off of me, oh my God. I can't believe what I saw! You left me!"

"Angie, what are you talking about? I'm right here! What is wrong? Why are you screaming?" he said.

I yelled, "Take me home!! Take me home!"

He replied, "Angie, I love you. Please stop this. You're scaring me!"

I rolled out of the car onto the heap of dirt and grass. I continued to scream and roll around in the dirt. I was crying and asking the Lord to forgive me!

He jumped out of the car and said, "Angie, ok, let me take you home. Why are you acting crazy? I can't take this. Please stop doing this. You are freaking me out!"

"You don't love me! The Lord is the only one who loves me. You are a liar! The Lord loves me! Why did you bring me here? Now look! I can't believe this happened!"

"Come on," he said. "Let me take you home then. Please get out the dirt."

As he tried to help me clean myself off and put my pants back on, I yelled at him. "Get your hands off of me! Don't you ever touch me again!"

I got back in the car and sobbed until I arrived home. He asked me what happened, and I told him that he would never understand.

"I can't ever see you again," I replied.

He watched me walk into the house after 2:30 am. I ran to the bathroom and jumped into my bed. My mother called out to me, but I didn't answer.

Finally, I said, "I'm home and going to sleep."

She decided to come into my room. She saw that I was crying and not ok. I told her that something had happened and that God wouldn't be pleased, but I stopped it. She assured me of God's grace and how it covered me when I made mistakes. I laid in her arms and cried. Eventually, I went to sleep.

I woke up that morning and refused to eat. I also cut the weave that I had in my hair. I wanted to start clean. I wanted nothing to do with the past. My real hair was long, so I washed and styled it. I stayed home for about three days, feeling extremely sorrowful for disobeying God, and for thinking my flesh was strong enough because I had never been with him in over 2 years. I put confidence in my flesh and was completely tricked by the devil. I totally forgot about the vision I had.

About two weeks later, I graduated from junior college and had already taken classes at a four-year university. At graduation, I felt sick, but I pushed through it. My taste buds were off, but I couldn't really identify what I was feeling. I walked around with maxi pads for three weeks, waiting for my period to come down.

At the time, I was working at a supermarket, but quit to work at my new job. I was a Community Technician. That was just a fancy way to say someone who supervised and took disabled and mentally challenged members out into the community while assisting them with their daily activities. As I was on the job one day, only two weeks into working there, I fell asleep standing up. Up until that point, I had only witnessed crack heads or people who were extremely high fall asleep while still standing.

How was that possible that I didn't even realize what I was doing?

No matter what time I went to sleep at home, I woke up exhausted. I even felt like I couldn't breathe. I was literally falling asleep butt naked. Everything around me smelled terrible. The new job I had smelled of coffee and spit! Everything I looked at made me want to vomit. Surely, my period was coming. So, as my supervisor called my name three times before I answered, I woke up feeling so embarrassed. He told me to go wash my face. As I went to the bathroom, I was greeted by an African woman. She told me I was pregnant and that I was going to have a baby boy. I told her I was just waiting for my period to come down. Then, I went into the bathroom stall. I just knew blood would come streaming down inside the toilet bowl, but there was nothing.

I was as dry as a horse.

I washed my hands, and the same woman told me that what she was saying was true. She said, "You will see."

I told her I hadn't had sex, so that wasn't true. The next day, I pressed my way back to work and felt terrible.

My final diagnosis to myself was that one of the members' saliva must have given me hepatitis or something. I decided to call my middle brother up. I asked him to take me to the hospital. So, he did, and also picked up my mother. This Indian male doctor wearing a turban had me take a urine test. As my mother and I were waiting for the results, he asked my mother to step out of the room. I told him it was ok to let her stay; however, he insisted on her leaving. So, she stood outside the curtain. That's when he broke the news to me.

He said, "You are pregnant. Why didn't you use protection?"

I told him he was mistaken. I told him to take a blood test as well. He assured me that there were high levels of potassium in my urine and that there was no need to do that. I told him that I wasn't having sex.

Then, it hit me.

He told me that the only way I could end up pregnant was to have sex. I covered my face, totally embarrassed, and proven to be a whole liar. I asked if he could ask my mother back into the room. He left out, and Mommy came back inside. I told her the news, and she said she suspected, especially when my taste buds were changing and I was sleeping naked. I reminded her of the night a month before, when I came home, crying from that experience. She remembered all too well. I told her, "But...Mommy... it was three pumps. He didn't cum, Ma. I stopped it! I pulled it out. We never finished, so how did I become pregnant?"

She replied, "Didn't they teach you in high school that you could get pregnant from precum?"

I just looked at her and cried. "I thought God knew I was sorry. We prayed, Ma. You told me that he forgave me and gave me his mercy. Doesn't he know that I made a mistake?"

"Yes, Hunny, he does," said my mother. "And he will see you through."

Now, I had to reach out to the very man who possibly ruined my life, as well as address my church. That meant shame, judgment, condemnation, etc... all from the people of Christ. I had to face my family and my friends. So many people would be disappointed in me. The biggest person of all – myself. No one would understand what really happened that day. Not the father, not my family or friends, and definitely not the church. They weren't concerned with the details of it all.

Here it goes with this negro, he came around less and less until it just ceased one day. He didn't have to deal with any of it. I had to face it all, and all did I face! No matter how many times I repeated this sad story, everyone laughed at me and said, "You really got pregnant off of three pumps?"

Out of all my pain, that was the thing that stuck out. Yes, sometimes I even laughed, at first, but then reality kicked in, and it was no joking matter. I was in so much pain emotionally. Then, it took a toll on me physically. I was fighting in a battle for my very life. Fighting spiritually and fighting physically. The father asked me what I was going to do, and I told him I was keeping my baby. It clearly wasn't in his plans. At first, he acted like he supported me. Then, he didn't show up to help me in and out of the hospital. So, I stopped calling him.

One day, he came over to the house after I came home from the hospital. This nutbag tried to feel me up and have sex with me. I couldn't believe him. I was sick as a dog, and all this man could think about was having sex! I told him to leave. Yes, I was sick, sick. Like, I was sick 24 hours a day, 7 days a week. I thought I was going to die!

I had **_HYPEREMESIS GRAVIDARUM_**!

This will remain one of the biggest battles of my life to date. I was fighting for my daughter's life and my sanity. I'm sure the quality of care is much different today than it was 20 years ago, so perhaps the suffering isn't as harsh. Let me tell you something! Nothing could have prepared me for this!

What in the world was happening to me? I remember waking up every day thinking that this feeling would leave my body, eventually. I thought pregnancy symptoms, at least the bad ones, would only last for a few months. I thought that if I threw up one time upon waking up in the morning, it would be all for the remainder of the day.

Not so! I was sick and miserable for six long months. I lost 20 pounds from either not eating or throwing up. I hated every smell, every taste...I was hot, then I was cold. My insides were sore, and it hurt to walk. The constant pressure on my bladder had me in so much pain. The dizzy spells occurred whenever I proceeded to walk. I would even have to rush to the bathroom since it was right next to my bedroom, but I would collapse on the floor before I could make it. I felt like I was absolutely dying. This wasn't living at all.

Why am I going through this suffering? God must be punishing me for sure! I don't know anybody who is or has been allergic to pregnancy. So yes, I thought that everything I was feeling must have been a curse sent from God. He had not forgiven me yet. This feeling went against anything I had ever been taught. God forgives all sins, except this one.

I was grief-stricken.

I had no drive.

I had no will to live.

I had no hope.

I was full of anguish and despair. Even the last time I spoke to that joker, whose name is "***sperm donor,***" he asked me if I was ready to be a mother. My response to him was, "I am already a mother." Then, in turn, I asked him if he was ready to be a father. He replied with another question to me.

He asked, "Are we gonna be together?"

I replied, "No, but you can be in the baby's life. I won't keep you from them."

At the time, I was about 3 to 4 months pregnant and had not yet had a dream that I was having a girl, nor had I had an ultrasound, which could reveal the sex.

He replied with something extremely shocking to me. "Well then, no. I'm not gonna be a father…if we can't be together," he said.

Being slick with my mouth, I replied quickly by saying, "Ok then, goodbye!"

I hung up, quick, fast, and in a hurry. At that moment, I knew that he definitely wouldn't be a part of our lives. He dropped off his deposit of sperm and bounced. No obligation and no responsibility at all. He had two other children he mentioned before, so I didn't understand. I didn't care to. All I knew was that I wasn't going to be one of those baby mothers who chased after a man in order for him to commit to take care of his child. I was determined to use all of my strength to focus on my health and my baby.

I still had yet to understand what was happening to me physically. Eventually, because of all the vomiting and not being able to keep food down, I ended up in the hospital. I was admitted 5 or 6 different times. The pills didn't work, the IVs were temporary, and I stayed dehydrated. The doctor recommended a catheter. One was surgically inserted from my arm to my heart. That lasted a couple of months, with a nurse coming over twice a week to change my bandages. I had to take one bag of vitamins, rotated with a bag of Phenergan, a liquid to stop the nausea. My life started to become normal again. I was able to laugh at the movies again. I was able to eat oatmeal and eggs without throwing up. I was able to drink water, and it stayed down. I started to test out other foods like ribs and fried chicken. Yes! All the foods I missed with flavor. My weight started to increase. Eventually, I had to go shopping because I didn't own any maternity clothes.

I remember my mother told me she believed that when a woman was pregnant, she was the most beautiful. So, she took me shopping and we purchased the cutest outfits. Things were looking optimistic for me – for me and my baby. I was still connected to my IV and a backpack for travel. I didn't care about the looks I received. Even in church, I felt the judgment. I felt the stares, but I continued to worship God and focus on his love that filled my soul. They would get over it soon, or risk getting cursed out in tongues.

One thing I was... I was protective of my unborn child. At that point, I refused to feel or allow my baby to feel any negativity. I had been through much – too much. So much so that a couple of months earlier, I went to the hospital, completely delusional. I was talking out of my head. The doctor gave me an option to abort, right there in the hospital. I walked in saying, "Ok, let's do it!"

She medicated me and told me that we would wait until the morning after I had rested, in order to make a clear decision. When the morning came, she walked in and asked me if I was ready to go upstairs for a DNC. I looked up at her like she had two faces.

I said, "I'M NOT KILLING MY BABY!"

She reminded me that it was an option because I said I couldn't deal with being pregnant any longer. So again, I told her that I didn't know what I was talking about. I also didn't know what a DNC was. I could barely walk coming into the hospital, much less make a decision like that. She let me know that was why we waited until I was hydrated and rested. She continued to be my doctor and the one who delivered my daughter. Her name was Dr. Susan Pitman. She was the best doctor I've ever had. I just knew she would deliver all my future children. Only thing is, I never had another baby.

As I continued to thrive from the help of the IV and the medicine, I was able to feel, look, and act normal. Some symptoms did not change, though. I still had this itching disorder going on. My legs and buttocks were darkened from the scratching. Both had welts and old scabs on them. I would wake up with blood running down my hips and legs. It felt like I had spiders and ants crawling up my legs all day and night.

Another symptom of Hyperemesis was spitting. I carried around a medicine spit jar, and it smelled foul! I went through so many of those. My mouth stayed watery or juicy with saliva. That pregnancy changed my entire life. However, even through it all, my baby was growing big and strong. She was healthy indeed. All that I had gone through never affected her. She continued to pull all the nutrients she needed from my body. I was the one who couldn't handle it.

When I was 5 months pregnant, the Lord gave me a dream because I started to worry about the sex of the baby. I started to worry because I wanted a boy really badly. I felt like I would be too hard on my baby if it were a girl. I feared it because of my upbringing. I didn't want my daughter to experience the things I had growing up. I thought I would worry less if I had a son.

One night, I had a dream that I had a baby girl, and she was light-skinned with hair sticking straight up. She looked like a baby bird. It was funny. I remember waking up crying, and I told my mother my dream. She assured me that it was time I got used to the fact that it wasn't going to be a boy, even though all I spoke about was having a son. That African woman at work also promised me I was having a son. Lying tongue is what that was, because my dream was vivid and real. I didn't have that physical knowledge until I had my second ultrasound. Indeed! I was having a girl, and I was excited because God showed it to me. So, I began searching for names.

One day early in my pregnancy, I needed to go somewhere. I don't remember where I was going, but I caught a connecting bus to go back home. I started to feel sick. Just walking was becoming painful. At this point, I already knew I was pregnant. Anyways, as I got off the bus, my old friend, whom I hadn't seen in a year or so, bumped into me as I was waiting for the second bus. She let me know who she had recently seen. She told me that she saw my baby's father at the Shoprite supermarket. He had picked her up from work to take her home. He was trying to come into her home to cook her breakfast. However, she refused and told him that he couldn't. She also let him know she was back with her ex-boyfriend. I was confused because I thought she was long gone and out of the picture since she left my home when I was 19 years old. Now, I was 22 and here she was again, telling me she had yet another encounter with the *sperm* **donor.**

Of course, she had no idea that he and I ever hooked up. She knew we were friends, but that was the extent of it. Then, I told her that I was pregnant with his baby. She was equally shocked. I had been in and out of the hospital for months, and this man was still trying to sleep with my old friend...whom he used to deal with. They were never a couple, but they had a sexual relationship. So she proceeded to tell me that he always calls her and tries to pick her up from work and take her home. What she also told me was that she had a baby with her ex and was going to have another one. She wanted nothing to do with my child's donor. She didn't understand why I even hooked up with him. She reminded me of how I told her that he was a womanizer and that I warned her about him.

I did remember that. However, after knowing him from 19 until 22 years old, I gave in once, and that episode shouldn't have even happened. I felt even more like a fool. I let her know that I should have taken my own advice. My bus was coming, and she wished me luck. I could tell that she was disappointed in me. Even though she didn't like him anymore, the fact remained. *How am I going to warn her about his behavior and then fall for the trap myself, knowing I knew better?* I was stupid, I was weak, and I was tricked. Tricked by the enemy. I was being set up the entire time. The devil had me right where he wanted me. I was ruined!

Boy! I couldn't wait until I arrived home. I stormed through my doors and screamed out my youngest brother's name!

"Wait 'til you hear this," I said. "Guess who I ran into? Guess what she told me?"

Then, I proceeded to tell him what she said.

He said, "Word? Get out of here. So, what you gonna do?"

I replied, "Imma call him and see what he says."

So, I did just that. I asked him if he saw the girl. Of course, he lied. Then, he said he saw her a long time ago and gave her a ride home because she didn't have a way. I asked him to come over, and he said he would come, but first wanted to know why I wanted to see him suddenly. The thing was, I barely called him. He wasn't supportive like a man expecting a new baby should be, so that turned me completely off from him. I only spoke to him when necessary. He refused to come until I told him the reason why I wanted him to come.

When I finally got tired of all the going back and forth, I told him to come over so I could ask him in his face and tell him the rest of all she told me. He refused. Then, I started to threaten him.

I said, "Don't be scared now. Bring your ass over here because the moment I see you, I'm going to bust your head open with a frying pan! How dare you try to play me when I'm trying to carry your baby, being sick and all? I'm in the hospital all the time, and you're cheating on me? Yeah, come on over here because I got something for you!"

Of course, he kept denying it. He told me that I was tripping and that he wasn't going to come. He hung up. My brother told me I was too upset and needed to calm down, but it was far too late to be calm. I wanted revenge, and I wanted it badly. As a matter of fact, I hated the fact that I was pregnant. I wished it would go away.

Two days later, I reached back out to him to let him know I had just come from the hospital because I had a miscarriage. My intention was to go on with my life and have absolutely no dealings with him. He started to cry, which was very shocking to me. He put on a good show because I knew he didn't care deep down. He asked me if I needed anything.

All of a sudden, he started to act like a concerned human being, knowing damn well he was relieved. He damn sure wasn't fooling me. He told me he needed to call me later. He said that he couldn't believe he lost his baby. The nerve of him trying to act like my pregnancy mattered to him now when he played like a ghost all this time. All this man ever wanted was sex, and getting it one time was not enough. We hung up, and I felt relieved to finally be rid of him. Being the kind of person I was, I knew it would take a day or two for my conscience to kick in. I told my mother and brother what I had done. They said it wasn't right, but of course, they understood. They understood that I said it because I was hurt at that time. I also realized the same.

So, I met with him across the street from his building. I borrowed my friend's car and parked it across the street at the park. When he got in the car, he acted like he missed me. He tried to kiss me, and I pushed him away. He asked me what I had to show him. At first, I hesitated. I was afraid of his response. He let me know that I could tell him. He said he still wanted to be with me. Then, I touched my belly and showed him with my hands that I was still pregnant. His face was shattered.

"How are you still pregnant?" he asked.

I told him, "I lied to you. I never lost the baby."

He yelled, "What!?"

He tried to get out of the car, but I pulled his arm back in and said, "Listen, this isn't about me and you. It's about the baby. I want you to be a father to the baby now that you know."

He asked me, "So, do you want to be with me?"

I said, "No, I don't."

He got out of the car, and I followed. I called out his name as he walked away. Then, he walked back into his building while I stood there looking all kinds of stupid. I was stupid. I allowed the enemy to use me and make matters even worse. I was hurt and angry at the same time. I knew he felt rejection, but the real truth was that he may have felt relief because he thought he was off the hook. I don't believe he ever wanted to be with me. He preyed on women for a living. I know many people may not feel like this was the case, but as time goes on, you will see how my instincts have always been right.

Sometimes you won't see it, but that feeling inside should never be ignored. I regret not listening to my soul. I regret putting any kind of confidence in this flesh. No, I didn't regret my daughter that I eventually had, but I regretted the sin that brought her here that way. She deserved to be loved by two parents in one household. I should have been married first. Those were the values instilled into me as a child.

At the age of 16, I remember saying that I did not want to ever be married. I said I wanted to raise a child on my own. *Who in their right mind would sign up to do this job alone?* There are many of us, apparently. However, there was a reason. Whatever trauma we as little girls experienced was enough to make us feel that raising our sons and daughters alone was the best thing.

It's the furthest from the truth. It needs to be the RIGHT MAN! Unfortunately, it wasn't. When he walked away that day, the next time I saw him was in court when my daughter was 7 weeks old. My mother made me apply for welfare, and I couldn't believe this was my life. I eventually got a job when my daughter was 8 months old, but to leave her with strangers at a daycare was the worst feeling ever. I was overly protective of my daughter. If I could help it, she would never ever feel pain, hurt, or rejection. This was too much pressure on me because that was something that I could not even avoid. Due to my sins, that may have been the first feeling she ever experienced...

REJECTION!

I tried to make it right by telling the truth, of course, after the lie. Honestly, I knew his response wouldn't permit him to stay around. At that point, God had already revealed to me that he wasn't going to be in the picture. So, my heart was already prepared, and I went on with my life. My illness became worse. I went back and forth to the hospital a lot. I had lost 19 pounds total, and I was now 120 pounds and 6 months pregnant. I looked extremely weak and feeble, but I was alive, though. Finally, I was able to hold food down. The day I had her, I was 139 pounds.

CHAPTER NINE: NOT AGAIN!

As I was going through the pregnancy, I attended church as much as I could. There was a visitor whose mother was a member of the church. He was a retired police officer, and he took a liking to me. I actually met him before I was pregnant; however, we never spoke. At this point, I was pregnant, but wasn't showing much. Our first conversation felt very strange. I didn't tell him I was pregnant at the time. One day, I was admitted to the hospital, and he came to visit me because he was worried about what was wrong with me.

Although at that time I was attracted to older men, he was much older than I was, so it was kind of gross in my opinion. He was way past the threshold. He was 35 or 36 years old, I believe. Anyways, he seemed not to know why I was in the hospital.

I asked him, "Do you know what floor you are on?"

He said, "I'm on the fourth floor."

"You're on the maternity floor."

"Oh," he replied.

"Yes, I'm pregnant, and no, I'm not with the father."

"Ok. Well, I still like you and I'm here."

I smiled because a friendship of any kind wasn't my focus, but he was surely there for me for as much as I allowed him to be. He took me out to eat, gave me money, and treated me kindly. The first time he kissed me, I was about 7 months pregnant. He waited for about 3 months to kiss me, and it never went past that. We never had sex, not until after my baby was born. We didn't even have a title. He was just a minister in the church who was helping me...I guess.

Eventually, I grew to love him. To my surprise, I met his daughter. I knew he had sons, except for one son whom he never spoke of. However, his daughter, who lived in Florida, was the one who told me about him. I was upset that he was withholding important information from me. Of course, there's always a story about the baby's mother... blah blah blah. I listened, but at that point it was too late. The trust we had established was gone.

He was much older, and I started to feel like I had my entire life ahead of me. Yes, he had a strong build, he was short and stocky, handsome, but he was older, and I couldn't get over that. I felt like being with an older man might slow me down from my goals. Plus, I was too young to be a stay-at-home mother, taking care of a husband

and kids. *Hell, could this man even ride a roller coaster with me?* I mean, we had good conversations and he showed me that he could be a good provider, although he was living in the basement of his mother's house... which I didn't understand all the way. He swore he was just saving money. That fact, I understood. He had plans to get a house down South. Years later, I think he did.

He furnished my brand-new baby's room with carpet. He and my sister also purchased a crib and dresser set. The room was unfurnished when I went into labor, and fully furnished when I arrived home from the hospital with the baby. I will forever be grateful for that. Eventually, he took me to meet some of his family in Florida and Georgia. We were all over the place. Here I was with a new baby and traveling back and forth with this man. When I went on dates, I was with him.

When we would go out, the only people I ever allowed to watch my daughter were my mother and my sister. Most times, they ended up watching her together because I still lived with my mother until my daughter was a year old. If we brought her with us, I would breastfeed her in the back seat of his car, and he would make sure we had everything we needed. Honestly, we felt like a family...we were a family. He was a stand-up guy who, for some reason, assumed the responsibility that her deadbeat sperm donor didn't. I mean, this guy bought my daughter milk, clothes, food, and so much more. There was nothing he didn't do for us, and he spent time with us.

Eventually, I went to court to file for child support and full custody of my daughter. *Can you believe this asshole was in the same elevator with me and didn't even look or ask to see his daughter?* Only thing he did was hold the elevator for us when it was time to get off. That was very strange to me. The older man I was seeing dropped us off and promised to wait for me outside. So, I was in court alone to face this monster of a man.

The judge had us announce our names, then proceeded to say that when it came to visitation, I needed to pump my milk and send my newborn off to be with him for the weekend. THE NERVE! I almost died!

"Excuse me, your honor, I only breastfeed and cannot do that."

This wicked judge told me that I had no choice but to put it in a bottle.

I was **HUMILIATED!**

Although I lied because I gave my daughter both breast and bottle, but my baby was only 7 weeks old. I just didn't want this non-existing nigga to have my baby for one second. He had given me nothing!

Lo and behold, the sperm donor had a suggestion. "Your honor, if it's ok with her, I can come over to her house and see the baby every weekend."

I know this dude didn't even own his own bed, much less a room for my daughter to visit. He lived with his great aunt, who was older than Jesus. There was no way my baby was going there! The judge turned to me and asked me if that was ok, and I immediately responded, "YES!"

She then told me to have the baby dressed and ready to see him on time. I smirked. *Was this woman serious? She's a joke. She can't even tell when a father isn't interested.* Then, she spoke about finances. This dude said he was on UNEMPLOYMENT!

WOW!

The judge awarded us both joint custody, and he had to give me $100 a week... or a month... I don't even remember which one because I never received it after all these years. I received paper checks in the amounts of $0.30, $0.15, $0.13, and $0.19. Basically, I received absurd amounts. It would take ten checks sometimes just to make $2.00. It was absolutely DISGUSTING! The most I received at that time was $11, and that was once a month. By the time she was nine years old, it went up to $19. I remember the first time I received $40. I could not believe it!

When my daughter was 11 years old, I took him back to court for an increase and bumped into one of his other baby's mothers. There was yet another child after my daughter. I will talk about how many more children I found out this man had in another chapter. Now, the number was up to nine kids – so I thought.

The judge increased my support, but after the new mother walked in, he decided to keep the support as it was. I was sick, but not as sick as this woman. She had the support of her sister and mother, but I was alone. It was yet another joke to me. I introduced myself to her, but she was not feeling me or what I was saying. I tried to encourage her to let our kids meet because they need each other, but she was against it. However, her mother took my phone number just in case she changed her mind in the future. She was in shock, especially after I told her how many other children he had and that there was more than what I knew.

She didn't fully understand why I was laughing. I told her I had been dealing with his absence and lack of support for years. This was simply his lifestyle. I assured her that whenever she changed her mind, my daughter would love to meet her sister. She assured me that she would never change her mind, and if her father wanted her to know, then he should be the one to tell her. I said ok, and I left it at that. I didn't end up hearing from her until a month after my sister died. At the time, my daughter was 14 years old.

As I continued my relationship with the retired cop, I became pregnant again. It must have been the first time he had sex with me because it had been four months since I had my baby. It was almost five months later when I discovered I was getting sick again. Those same symptoms came back. If you ask me, I was allergic to pregnancy.

I remember being at his place and lying on his bed. He said to me that he knew I was curious about how *it* felt with him. I told him that I was ok. Up until this point, he had never tried anything with me. Now, it was *clearly* time to pay up. He started kissing me and I enjoyed it, but became nervous because I remembered what happened to me before when I wasn't ready or expecting it. He told me he only wanted to feel it for a second and that I would be ok. Once we started, I told him that it was enough because we didn't have protection. I remember him telling me that he did have it, but he just wanted me to see how it felt. Then, he stopped.

Just like that.

I looked at him in utter confusion. I looked like a deer caught in headlights, or a sad puppy. I was looking for an explanation as to what happened. It was very strange. He held me, assured me that I was ok, and told me that he wanted me to feel a sample of what it would be like. I remember putting my hands in my underwear and touching my wetness.

"Did you cum?" I asked because I felt gooey and sticky.

"I was nowhere near climaxing!" he responded.

I was still not convinced. *Was this what sex would be like? Was I supposed to feel nervous and scared every time?* I did not like the negative feelings connected to being intimate. Something so beautiful was tainted with sin, which made it horrible.

I knew better!

He knew better, especially seeing as though my baby was four months old. That was the last thing I needed – another one so soon. I tried to keep in mind that he was a minister of the gospel, but no! What he was at that very moment was a horny man, and I was submitting to my wifely duties, without the ceremony. All the guilt and the shame associated with sin and fornication made me fall ill. I wanted to be alone. For some reason, it was hard for me to process that this was all he wanted, even though all men were interested in it.

All these months had passed, and now we do it?

Why weren't we getting married first...since were are playing house?

Yes, he was a good man, according to my standards.

Wait! Did I even have any standards?

I was questioning who I was. I couldn't blame it all on him. Once again, I opened my legs. I wasn't a 15-year-old little girl anymore. This was my life, and I needed to say what's next. I needed to call the shots. *So, why was I taking the lead from some man?*

Clearly, I had insecurity issues. My character was flawed. I didn't understand who I was or what I was supposed to have and protect as a woman. I gave him the very thing I was only beginning to discover...my sense of womanhood. It was the only thing that seemed to make him happy, and it had been months. We had good conversations, and I was a wonderful mother, but I wasn't his wife, which made it wrong. As always, the promises of security and control of my future were always followed in conversation. He promised me that he was there to stay and that he knew how to take care of me. I guess that was to let me know he wasn't a fly-by-night kind of guy.

Two weeks later, I found myself in the same position with him. This time, I told myself this was it. This had to be the way. At that point, I couldn't say I loved him, but I didn't know what else to do. I was 23 years old and was dating a 36-year-old man. He was the one winning. He could mold me and make me into whoever he wanted me to be. Things were going so fast for me. I didn't know what was coming or going...talk about going with the flow.

His mother noticed how much time we were spending together. She made a comment to us both. She said, "If you play with fire, you will get burned."

She was also a member of my church. When you're an adult, you feel like you don't need instructions because you have it all under control. Unfortunately, the devil lies waiting for an opportunity to jump right in when your guard is down.

I never thought I was a weak woman. I was sassy with my mouth and always stood up for myself, but for some reason, the acceptance of the men I dated was important to me. So much so, I would throw my own values away. I really didn't understand the power of sex. I didn't understand the responsibility I had to take and own as a woman. *Yes, it's my body, but why did I keep giving it away to unworthy and careless men?* They were only concerned about their needs. Not once was I ever accounted for. They were ready for it, so it was my *duty* to surrender and not fight. It was for me to say yes, before I even knew what I was doing. I was the one receiving their gift of life inside of me, without my consent.

I was too much of a coward to say, 'Wait!' or 'This is too much for right now.' I was just speechless. In utter confusion, I waited for something to happen. I waited for the fireworks to go off so I could wake up. Well, they went off alright. They popped in my ears in a whole other way. As I explained, two weeks later, in the same place, it was a different story.

I was all in.

I mentally decided, this was *my du*ty. I asked him to use a condom, but he ignored me. This time was the real deal. He was a powerful and strong man. He turned me upside down in that room. I was shocked because I had never been handled in such a way. When he picked me up and started to pound me out, I was lost for words. I didn't know what was going on. This time, it lasted much longer, but when did he cum?

He lied.

He told me he didn't.

Suddenly, he stopped and he began to pray for our sin.

WHAT IN THE HELL!!!

Did this nigga just stop to pray? Now, I was really confused and lost. *Will this be the experience every time?* I asked him what was wrong. His response was that he felt convicted. He knew God saw us, and as a minister, he was leading us in the wrong direction. So, I agreed and we stopped. We never did it again until we went to Florida, which was about three weeks later, when we were visiting his distant relatives.

I remember that I was extremely tired, and I felt extremely ill. One of his family members gave me lasagna. I tried to eat it, but the amount of oil and butter it had, along with excessive amounts of cheese, made me run to the bathroom to throw up. I actually wasn't able to hold anything down. He made a joke about me being pregnant, and it wasn't funny at all.

The next day we went to see his cousin's house that he had built. His home was very huge and beautiful. Compared to the prices of homes today, his home and land were cheap. Then, the older guy started talking about building and moving down south, but he wanted to know if I was willing to raise a family there. I told him that I would go wherever my *husband* wanted to go.

When we went back to relax at his cousin's house, we ended up talking in the bedroom. This would be the last time we fooled around. I felt really, really sick, and I told him that I thought I was pregnant for real. His response to that was to have sex with me again, saying there was no sense in holding back since I was pregnant anyway. He made love to me quietly and told me that he wanted to marry me.

On our way back home to New Jersey, I felt terrible. I also had my baby to carry and take care of this time, so it was even harder than the first. As she slept, a song came on the radio.

Lo and behold, another *Maxwell song*.

It was titled, "LIFETIME." He sang about letting your life pass you by. He also sang about taking it one day at a time, spreading your wings, and flying. If you want it, you can have it, just believe. It was my choice. At that very moment, I felt that if I married this man, I would be trapped. I would be marrying him for the wrong reasons. I wouldn't be marrying him for love. I had my whole life ahead of me. I sat in the backseat with my baby, who was asleep, and I just wept. I couldn't believe I let myself get messed up – again. I still had not learned my lesson. I was sick physically, but my soul was in agony.

My soul was in complete despair.

My soul lacked hope.

My soul was rotten!

What have I done!

The next day after we returned home, we sat down and broke the news to my mother. I told her we would be getting married soon, but she didn't understand why. So, I broke the news to her that I was pregnant. She was speechless. He told her that he would take care of me. Funny enough, I don't remember her full response. I do know, privately, she let me know that he was a good man, but older, and asked me if I was sure.

I responded, "No, I'm not sure, but what choice do I have?"

She reminded me that I already had a baby. I could tell she was disappointed in my actions. Honestly, the days to come were getting harder and harder, so I relied heavily on my mother and sister, who wasn't too well herself, to help me care for my daughter. The same exact thing happened to me when I was pregnant with my first baby.

This was unbelievable! This can't be my life! What in the heck is wrong with me? It seemed as if I couldn't have, let alone enjoy, sex without getting pregnant. What I did know was that I was really allergic to pregnancy! I especially believed this to be so because I didn't know anyone personally who went through this. I had never known this was something that only 2% of women dealt with. Yet, I was a part of that 2%, and I got the privilege of having all the symptoms. Just so happen, I was also supposed to be a child of God.

My heart was always right, but when sin comes in, I believe every believer gets it worse. This was definitely me reaping what I had sown. However, I felt the punishment to be way too harsh. In fact, this time I wasn't willing to pay the price. I just couldn't! Eventually, my family had to take me to the hospital, and just like before, I was admitted. When my mother and sister brought my baby to me two days later, I was in shambles. I had never spent the night away from my daughter.

Not ever!

It was the worst feeling ever. They said that she was okay, but I was a mess. I needed my baby. I needed to be her all in all. They gave her to me to hold, but I was so weak that I didn't have the strength to hold her. I cried! I couldn't believe this was happening to me. My life was far from a pretty picture. It was a picture full of *chaos*. Chaos that I created from my broken heart. My inability to deal with my childhood trauma and rejection caused this very moment.

Why was I with an older man?
Why was I pregnant for the second time?
Why was I trapped?
How in the world can God turn this story around?
I didn't think he could.

I did not trust that this Heavenly Father would do any more than my Earthly father could. Hell, my Earthly father disappointed me. I blamed him for the state of my mind and soul. Had he loved me in the right way, I wouldn't be in all this pain now. I would be able to sniff bad men out like the ones I had involved myself with. I would have felt special had I received love from my father. I would have felt important enough to care for *ME* first. I would have known what it meant to love myself.

Why was anything and anyone acceptable for me? I had not created any boundaries for myself. Therefore, I was falling into all kinds of mess. I proclaimed Christ, yet my sins stayed before me. The things of the world looked more promising than God's provision for me. Sin causes a person to be dark and angry. Yet, unforgiveness turned my heart into acid, and I was looking for someone to wash away the years of resentment. I was looking for outside factors to make me whole as a woman...as a person...as if I even knew what wholeness felt like. All I was doing was self-destructing, and now I was bringing another life into my madness.

What am I going to do now?

I was released to go home because there was nothing the hospital could do for me. I was told that I needed to follow up with my doctor and resume the same care I received with my daughter. Only thing different was that I couldn't see the same doctor. I previously shared the same insurance with my mother. Now, I was of age, and my mother's insurance no longer covered me. In fact, my daughter and I were on Medicaid, so I needed to choose a doctor under their plan. If anyone ever had welfare or Medicaid, they would tell you there was nothing like having your own personal doctor. The professionalism and concern towards the patient were the complete opposite of what it should be. Those Medicaid doctors get paid whether or not they look at you as a messed-up charity case. They would see you for a total of three minutes tops, and rush you out of their office without answering any of your questions.

I absolutely hated it. I wasn't willing to go through that torment and shame. I was hopeful that whatever I was going through would be different this time. So, another week passed and my mother had to go back to work. My sister had to go home to her husband, and I had to resume caring for my daughter, which I could barely do. The older guy had to come over and help me with her, but it wasn't the same. I still couldn't pick her up, and I could barely change her diaper. Every day my mother returned home, I was relieved.

He and I spoke about the future.

I remember him saying, "Stop thinking that just because you're pregnant, I don't want you. I still want to be with you, Angie."

I didn't believe him. I think he may have loved me, but I also felt like he was just taking responsibility for what he had done – what *we* had done. If I weren't pregnant with his child, he would not have asked me to marry him so soon. I think he only wanted to because of what others may have said about us. It was because of the shame it caused, but I didn't want to get married for any other reason than love.

The amount of stress and pressure I felt was unreal. I believe my mental state was far worse than my physical. I needed to make a decision quickly. Later that week, I was throwing up and could barely walk. I needed help to do everything. I told my man that I couldn't take it anymore and that I needed to end this pregnancy. He told me he didn't want to do the same, but he would support me. So, he drove me to the clinic, walked me inside, and asked me if I was going to be okay. We both were silent after that, then my name was called, and he waited outside in his car.

When they were doing the abortion, I woke up SCREAMING, "NO!"

I remember that moment so vividly. They held one of my arms down and stabbed a needle into it. Then, I drifted back under. Later, when I woke up with heavy cramping and feeling nauseous, they gave me a grape-flavored Tootsie Roll lollipop. I will never forget that. I ate it and it was tasty. I also had a huge bruise on my arm from where they stabbed me with the needle.

It wasn't a dream. It really happened.

My mind wouldn't let me rest, even under anesthesia. My heart really didn't want to do it, but I felt like I had no other choice. The older guy came up the back stairway to walk me down to the car.

As we drove away, he said, "I wanted to stop you, but you were minutes away from feeling relief, so I couldn't say anything. I wanted to tell you that we could have worked together to make this work. You didn't have to do that. I would have taken care of you."

I looked at him and cried. I said, "I couldn't hold the baby I have. I just want to go home and hold my baby."

We remained silent. He dropped me off at home, and we said our goodbyes. He checked on me later, but I didn't want anything more to do with him or any man for that reason. I was tired of being the one to get stuck with the problem. I was tired of messing myself up because of the ways a man would lie to me. Even if the lie was for a moment, it always boiled down to one thing, and that was sex. Nothing after sex was important.

Is this what relationships are supposed to be like?
I wanted no more parts of it. We talked less and less.

Then, I started reading a book by T.D. Jakes, called *Daddy's Little Girl*. This book changed my perception. It also assisted in my healing. It explained a lot about my relationship with my father. I felt like I could finally take responsibility for my actions and my future. This wasn't the end of my life like I thought it was. I got up the courage to tell the older guy that I no longer wanted to see him. I told him that what we had done turned my heart completely off, and I could no longer go forward with him knowing our secret. I needed to start off fresh, and I wanted to leave those skeletons in the closet. He said that he understood and was willing to respect my wishes. He also told me that if I needed anything that he would be there for me. Shortly afterwards, he moved away.

I never saw him again until years later at Staples. I was 42 years old at that time. He was with his oldest son. He wanted me to give my mother his mother's number because, at some point in time, she must have inquired about my mother. I said my goodbyes and left the store. He was much older now, of course. As I walked away, the reminder of the baby we shared crossed my mind. That was a memory I wished never existed.

After I had that abortion, my sister gave me a card with a Tweety bird on it. It was so adorable. Inside, it said that I would get through this and how *LIFE GOES ON*. Indeed, it went on. Before I knew it, my daughter was a year old, and I was looking for my own place to live. I had been working since my daughter was eight months old. My mom had been renting out this house in Irvington, New Jersey, and she was ready for us all to go our separate ways. My mom also purchased a car that we both shared, which made it much easier for us to get around.

I remember when the drug dealers on the block would mock and make fun of me struggling with my daughter. They would tell me that I wouldn't have to take the bus if I were their lady. They would laugh and ask me if I needed help in the cold. Every morning and afternoon, I would rush past them in an attempt to get home without hearing their stupid comments. So, when we got the car, I felt more than happy to drive past them.

Life was just that...life. It keeps going and stops for no one.

I could never manage to catch up. It felt like my life was getting nowhere. I was still struggling. I was still living in a tough neighborhood, even though I didn't hang around in that same neighborhood because I always kept to myself. I did work in an urban neighborhood where poverty was all around me. However, I never felt poor. Maybe in comparison to other people, but definitely not because of a lack. The Lord supplied all of my needs and some of my wants. I just felt stuck. I didn't know what I was supposed to do with my life. So, I got another boyfriend. Now, I was dating someone I really liked. It was someone I had always had a crush on for years. I couldn't believe we were actually a couple. Well, at that time, we didn't really label what type of relationship we had. It just was.

I was working as a teacher's assistant at this school. I had a boyfriend who was a probation officer or something like that. Most importantly, I had a beautiful daughter. I was on my way to moving into my own apartment and becoming more independent. I guess this was what *living* was. My boyfriend and I were both raised in the church, so we knew God. We even went to his grandmother's church together sometimes. He was a decent guy. He played the drums, and he rarely got into trouble, at least not street trouble. However, he already had a daughter whom I only saw twice, and according to him, he was no longer involved with his baby's mother. We went out to parties, and I would even stay the night with him sometimes. I rushed home in the mornings before my daughter woke up, though. I was always there to see her beautiful smile, and to smell her morning milk breath. I felt as though I was doing okay for a 24-year-old.

Until one day, my boyfriend kept acting stressed and started pushing me away. He wasn't really going out with me anymore, and we talked less. Then, I pulled away. He didn't like that much at all. I asked him to please tell me what was going on. This man opened his mouth and finally admitted to getting his baby's mother pregnant ***AGAIN!***

I was in shock. I just could not believe it.

This other woman was about four or five months pregnant, and this man had not spoken a word of it to me. He said that he thought she was getting rid of it months ago, like she said, but she decided to keep it. I asked him the details of how that even came to be, seeing as though I was seeing him for over five months. He said that it was the beginning of our friendship. He was going to see his daughter, and the child's mother lured him in with only a nightgown on. She didn't have any panties on. As he sat on the couch, after he put his then 2-year-old to bed, she sat on his lap. That's how she got pregnant. He swore he was never *with* her again, but I was confused because he told me that they didn't even get along with one another. He spoke very ill of her. He definitely had me believing there was nothing going on.

"So now this woman is pregnant!" I yelled.

I told him that he hurt me badly and I wanted nothing to do with him ever. I actually left him alone for a while. He ended up calling me and begging me to talk to him for about two weeks, give or take. I finally listened to him and decided to see him again.

Why did I do that?

I had moved into my own place and had more freedom. Although I didn't bring anyone home, I partied on weekends. I either dropped my daughter off at my sister's house or had my mom come over to watch her, but I always came back home. I never stayed out for days. My daughter saw me every morning. I was just having fun with my cousins and friends. When I didn't have to work, I turned up by drinking alcohol.

I remember having a good 'ole time with my boyfriend. My daughter was two years old and about to turn three. She was still in daycare. I was doing the normal hustle and bustle of life. Then one day, while sitting on my couch, my boyfriend told me that his baby's mother was going to have the baby soon and that he would be missing in action. Honestly, I had totally forgotten about her. I was pissed again. He assured me that he loved me. He said it was hard on him because he didn't want his kids growing up without a father. He was very stressed out, and it was taking a toll on our relationship. I told him I couldn't do it any longer. He had sex with me one last time on my couch. I was on top, and it felt better than it ever did. He told me to stop, and I thought I did. He said he didn't cum... as they all say.

Lies and more lies.

All I knew was, I didn't want to see him anymore. I stopped for about two weeks so he could go take care of his other business. The next call he received from me was that I was pregnant. Yes, I was now pregnant, along with his baby's mother. He didn't like that news at all.

He said, "I have two women about to have my baby?"

I responded with, "I guess so."

My plan was to keep the baby. I even told a couple of my friends. In fact, I was getting sick at the school I worked at, and one of the teachers had an extra pregnancy test that she gave to me. I was throwing up and all, I couldn't eat, I was feeling horrible all day long, and this nigga was nowhere to be found. I took the test and cried the blues about being pregnant...*again.* I told my brother's baby mother about it because she knew my ex-boyfriend. She later called him, told him I wanted to get an abortion, and asked if he would pay for it. He said he didn't have the money at that time, and he would give it back to me when he did. Of course, he lied and never gave it back to me.

    I eventually spoke with him, and he said, "I thought you were going to keep it."

    "Yes, I wanted to, but seeing as though I'm sick and have missed work because of it, I can't. Not to mention, you are having another baby now. What do I look like being last on the list while you take care of your other family? I swear I want nothing to do with you. Just give me the money back."

    He said he would, but never answered again when I called him. Actually, he never called to check on me. My friends at the job, even older teachers, told me to get rid of the baby. I must have told a few of them I was keeping the baby, or else no one would have given me their opinions and encouraged the abortion. Everyone told me not to ruin my life. I still believe that had I not been so sick, I would have two children today.

    However, that wasn't the decision I made. Round two began, and I was sucking on another Tootsie Roll lollipop.

    I was in a dark place...extremely dark.

    I was ashamed, bitter, hurt, resentful, lonely, and I did everything except run into the arms of God.

    I tried to make sense out of all these broken and dysfunctional relationships, but I couldn't. They served no purpose in my life. I hadn't gained anything. I hadn't learned anything. So, I just kept repeating this vicious cycle, especially with this last man that I knew I loved and served well. It never seemed to be good enough. I was dealing with people who came with a load of crap themselves.

    I was dealing with men who didn't know their identity either. They were just sitting around spreading their seeds for sport. They had no idea of what true commitment was, and they all just claimed a woman temporarily until it didn't fit in their lives anymore. I loved hard until there was nothing left to love. If a man showed me that all he wanted was to be with other people, or to make my life more complicated than it already was, that meant he for damn sure didn't love me enough. Therefore, he was not deserving of my love or loyalty. I wasn't a big cheater. However, if I felt the man I was dealing with was on some sneaky shit, then I was on mine. Sometimes, I got a head start. When it was over with *him*, the best way to forget about *him* was to move immediately on to something better.

So, as I pondered what importance this last man had, I realized that this was the boyfriend who gave me the information about my child support, or lack thereof. He worked with another county, but had access to the information I needed. He was a probation officer. I told him about the low amounts of child support checks that I received, and against his job policy, he investigated it for me. I was grateful! He called me as I was working and asked me to come over after work. When I showed up, he handed me a list of other baby mothers' names and the amount of child support they were also receiving. I could not believe what I was reading.

"So, you mean to tell me this is the reason why I barely get anything for my daughter? He has 8 kids! Are you kidding me?"

He responded, "Yea babe, I'm sorry, but this is why you don't really get anything. They split it up between you all, and there's nothing left. He probably doesn't even know how much you get."

"I can't believe I was with someone who has all these children. He never told me this. I only knew about two of them. OMG! I feel so disgusting! Do you know the diseases I could have right now? I just can't believe this!"

"You have to keep this to yourself because I could get into a lot of trouble giving you this information."

"This won't get into the wrong hands. I needed to know this. Thank you!" I replied gratefully.

"Yeah, and now you can stop stressing over it. Now you know the truth. I didn't want to tell you because it's crazy. We see cases like this all the time. Plus, I figured that must have been the reason."

I hugged him and cried. He embraced me. So, if anything came out of our encounter together for 8 months, it was this pivotal information.

I took this good information and first shared the sad news with some close family members and friends. Then, I decided to take it a step further.

Why should my daughter be a secret? Not if I could help it!

She is important too.

So, I did what any mother would have done. I reached out to every mother on that list. It was about six or seven women. It was absolutely ridiculous! It pained me to do it, but I felt like I had no choice. My silence was killing me. That information about all these siblings was driving me nuts. I wrote a three or four-page letter to each of them. They were scattered everywhere. They seemed to be in every state. All the way from New Jersey, where we resided, to California. It was a mess!!

I waited for a couple of weeks until I received a response. I received calls from only four women. One was named Mona. She was older than I was, and she used to work with the *sperm donor*. They worked at a bank. Then, he moved in with her when she became pregnant. After the baby was born, she came home one day, and he was gone. She knew he moved out because his stuff was gone. I don't know if he communicated with her at all. I just know she didn't know his whereabouts. He definitely didn't have a relationship with his son Brien. She only had one child, and it was from him. She was a very pleasant woman, to say the least.

Then, there was another whose name I won't mention. She was cool. She actually came over to meet my baby and introduce her to her older sister. 'Til this day, they have a wonderful relationship. However, there was a huge gap where they didn't see one another. They met when my daughter was two years old, and her sister was about six. Then, they saw each other maybe three times after that.. It ended there, until they reunited when my daughter was 17 years old.

There was one that reached out to me from California. She claimed to be the first one to have his child. She thought I was crazy! She actually said that I was crazy, and she knew where I was raised, to clearly have the courage to reach out to so many different women. I told her it wasn't about me and my pride, but I reached out because I wanted my daughter to know her siblings. I grew up having a big family, so I didn't know what it was like to be alone. There was always someone around. I knew I didn't plan on having any more children at the moment, so I didn't want my daughter to miss out on the opportunity to build meaningful relationships with her siblings. That wasn't fair to her. If it were up to the donor, she would never be mentioned. I would have been damned if I allowed that to happen!

Anyway, this woman from California was funny. We spoke for about an hour or so. She told me about a time when they lived in a shelter together because her mother kicked her out when she got pregnant. I guess he didn't have a place to call home then, either. So, they lived in a shelter together for some time. Eventually, they went their separate ways. I believe she went back home and moved far away. He didn't even know she had given birth to his son. She was the baby's mother who received the bulk of the child support. She had a new relationship and was pregnant at the time I spoke with her. I wished her well. We planned to speak with one another again, but because of the distance, we both lost contact. All I remembered at that time was that she had a son who was about nine or 10 years old, and his name started with an S.

Then, here came the ratchet one! The kind of woman everyone dreads. She was so ghetto it wasn't funny. I lived in the hood as well, and I was *hood* with all the incorrect speech and lack of manners, but she was a different type of *ghetto*. When she called me in an attempt to get me "*straight*," every other word was a curse. She was toxic as HELL! I could understand why she was alone. She barely let me speak. Eventually, I just told her to crumble up the letter and forget she ever spoke to me.

This woman lived 15 minutes away from me, literally. Another baby's mother lived about five minutes away from me. This entire situation was overwhelming.

I tried to listen to her as she said, "Who are you and how you know my address? I don't play that! I don't know who the fuck you think you are! I asked him who you were and he said, you said you ain't have no baby. He said he only got one daughter named Michaela. What the HELL you want from me?"

I responded, "Yes, he does know because I told him when she was born. He's lying. Anyways, I wrote the letter to you because I want my daughter to know her siblings. This isn't about him. But you're not gonna keep cursing me out just for reaching out to you. If you don't want them to meet, then just say that and forget I ever contacted you. It's not important how I know where you live. A good friend helped me out."

"No, that's not right. Nobody is supposed to be giving nobody address out!"

"I know that!" I yelled.

As I proceeded to hang up, she began telling me that she was the first to have his kids. She had a girl and a boy named after him. I can't even repeat the name if I tried. Then, she asked them if they wanted to meet their baby sister in the background. They said they didn't care. So, I tried to arrange the meet-up, but she always had some excuse as to why they couldn't. When I called the second time, she told me one of the kids was graduating and it wasn't a good time. I stopped calling, and she never called me again.

That was a sad case.

The Puerto Rican mother, whom my daughter met her daughter three times, took me directly to the ***sperm donor's*** mother's apartment. She, my baby, and I knocked on her door. She opened up and was surprised! She embraced me and my daughter, but she didn't know anything about her. She didn't see too many of her grandchildren at the time. She battled with illness and was raising her oldest son's daughter from birth. Her hands were completely full. I tried my best to keep a relationship with her and my daughter. It lasted for a while, then it was no more. She became my daughter's Nana... his mother liked to be called that. She moved away to live with him, his wife, and other children in Texas. She only stayed a couple of years, then came back to reside in Jersey. Eventually, we reconnected and resumed our relationship. However, my daughter wasn't as fond.

She resents the fact that she is his mother and condones his behavior, but that's the furthest from the truth. You can't control your adult children. Good and bad decisions are on them. Once you raise them, it's for them to follow the right path. Either way, her Nana understands and does not force my daughter to accept her. She just prays that one day it will turn around and she will accept her love for her. I tried to tell her about important things and events that occurred in my daughter's life.

When we would go visit her Nana, there would always be pictures of her grandkids hanging on all the walls and her refrigerator. There were many pictures of my Mikaylah and pictures of the other Michaela. Spelled differently, but pronounced the same. You mean to tell me he has another daughter who is three years older than my daughter, half white, and has the same name? This story just kept getting bigger and more and more grotesque as the days went by.

I'M DONE!

At this point, I was totally at a loss for words. I had to look at myself and ask why I continued to connect myself to empty wells. I never felt like I was looking for a father figure, but I feel as though everyone looks in different places for love. There is nothing wrong with that. We are made to love and form healthy relationships. We were made to form healthy soul ties. It's the wrong ones that bring harm to us. The Bible tells us to guard our hearts above anything else, for the issues of life flow out of it.

We don't guard anything.
We don't guard our bodies.
We don't guard our minds.
Most importantly, we surely don't guard our hearts.

We trust everybody, and we allow anything inside of us. I should be speaking for myself, but I know so many people, both male and female, who have fallen prey to their emotions. Of course, no one goes into a relationship thinking they will be hurt. It's usually when you're in the middle or at the end of coming out of a relationship that you realize it was the worst decision you ever made. Nothing will ever be perfect. Sometimes, opposites do attract.

So, what exactly is the issue?
Is it about your purpose in their lives? I really don't have that answer.

Could the problem be me?
Was I reading the signs wrong?

Spiritually, I was never right for the men I connected myself to. I cared more about pleasing them than Christ. I wish I were more faithful to God and had created and kept my Christian standards. I regretted compromising my faith.

Did it mean they didn't know how to love me because they didn't understand how Christ loved the church?

It very well could be possible. However, not everyone is a believer. Sometimes, falling in love has nothing to do with religion. Because I was called out from the very beginning, God had already prepared whom I was to connect with.

What does that mean? It means that whatever my purpose was, and whatever direction God had for my life, he ordained a special person who would coincide with my future and the will he had for my life. When we step outside of that will and fall into temptation by the devil, we settle for things we would never have otherwise. It causes us to fall to our own evil desires. We dive deep into those things that bring instant gratification to satisfy the flesh. We never consult with the Lord. If we did, he would spare us so much heartache and headache.

Sometimes, what he chooses for us, we don't want. I threw back so many potentially good and Godly men to gain what I was attracted to. They all were decent-looking men, but nothing attracted me to them on a deep level. There was no chemistry, but I know that God could have changed that in the future. Then, there were the men I started off with, and when we got really spiritual, I discontinued our relationship. I tried to make them come over to my side after I had already given them a taste of the apple. I was a terrible witness. I was killing my witness. I could have been winning souls for the kingdom, but instead, they fell deep for me. I slept with them, and then played a good Christian girl. I was getting it all wrong. The times when I decided to take a stand for Christ, the men would go running. I should have let them run because that was a sign that they were never for me and had no interest in the Lord.

Sure, they love that you have faith and can pray *Hell* out of them. Sure, they enjoy your faith language and how you're so committed that you're too holy to cheat on them. However, the minute you introduce that same Christ that they admire inside of you, they claim not to need him. If you continue to push the issue of your God, they accuse you of judging them and changing all of a sudden.

Growing up, I was very confused about what was acceptable and the right thing to do. I didn't know how far was *too far*. My father was the complete opposite of my mother. It was ok for them to be unequally yoked.

Why did it have to be any different for me?

I needed to meet God for myself. My identity needed to be in him only. Loving and finding a man shouldn't have been my goal. Loving the lord and building up his kingdom should have always been my focus. In a perfect world, I could focus on that. However, we live in a fallen world. The temptations and distractions of this world are real. The devil is real. He is not to be played with. We will not and cannot defeat him unless we walk in the wholeness and fullness of God. We have to be holy, for he is holy.

My problem was that I was allowing imposters to trick me into thinking that was the love of God.

My true father.

Had I experienced true love from my earthly father, I would have been able to recognize the falseness. I wouldn't have wasted years of emptiness. These men were broken just like me. Most, if not all, the men I dealt with didn't know their fathers or have a relationship with them. Some were dead, on drugs, in jail, or had just abandoned them. They were raised by grandparents or their great-aunts. Some were raised in a single-parent household, where their mom was working all day. They resumed the responsibility of the man of the house. All they knew was how to take care of their siblings, fighting for their worth, school, and then getting a girl pregnant without marrying them. So, the cycle continued.

Where was the love?
Where was God in the middle of this chaos?

I knew my childhood was dysfunctional. So, when you hook up with someone equally dysfunctional, it's nothing more than a bomb ready to explode. I couldn't help him, and he couldn't help me. It was all his fault, but it was all my fault, too! I needed to be complete in order to offer anybody anything. I should've never entertained any men who weren't complete. I did not wait patiently for the Lord, for him to do the necessary work. The work of tearing down my idols. Those things, I built in the place of my relationship with him.

I spent so many years blaming God for allowing the hurt and pain in my life. Instead of allowing him to heal my heart and redirect my life, I chose my methods to self-destruct. That felt more beneficial at the moment. In the long run, it left me alone, sad, and even more bitter. God had to tear down everything, then rebuild the walls of my heart.

CHAPTER TEN: NEVER SAY NEVER

Never say never! There was a lot of stuff I used to say that I would never do. I learned slowly but surely that I had to eat those same words I spoke.

I would never drink alcohol... Did it.

I will never have an abortion... Did that.

I will never sleep with someone's husband... Did that too because I justified them being separated.

I will never turn my back on God... Definitely rejected him.

I will never kill someone... I haven't, but I want to sometimes.

I would never attempt to commit suicide... I tried, but since I'm writing, it shows I was unsuccessful.

I would never do drugs...I smoked weed a few times and enjoyed edibles.

I would never prostitute, but came damn near close.

I would never be with another woman because I didn't like it, but curiosity and pain definitely killed the cat.

The point is, don't ever turn your nose up at someone or say you would never do something. The same things you may have judged someone for doing could become the very thing you entertain, eventually. Until you have walked in their shoes, you don't have the right to judge lest you be judged. Instead, show some compassion and mercy because that's what God has extended unto us. We are not above anyone. Given the same circumstances, we may fall too. There is not enough time in the world for us to do everything we are big enough to do. I regret doing a lot of things. Even though I couldn't erase the mistakes I made, I decided that I could do better with my choices going forward. No longer would I continue in the cycle of dysfunction. It would only lead to a stagnant life.

You would think that after all of the drama and secrets, I was ready to turn back to Christ. After the abortion, I went into a dark shell. It does something to the inside of a woman. You just can't get your heart right. I started to view life as pure evil. I believed that everything I did was a trap. I tried very hard to do the right thing, but I wasn't rewarded for the good things I did. It was only the bad things that got attention. I have always lived a life where I minded my own business. The bullshit just had a way of finding me. I would go to work and keep to myself, but everything the devil does is strategic.

EVERYTHING!

For once, I made it out of something. I escaped this next situation only because of the mercy of God. I was working as a teacher's assistant at a Charter School. This security guard was reading this book by a black author that seemed intriguing. I asked him what he was reading and he told me what the book was about.

After he finished, he allowed me to read it. That was the start of reckless thinking. I started to go into deep imagination. The teacher I was working with at the time would call my name, and I would be gone in my thoughts. I was reading books that had crime, sex, and money.

All the things that make the world go round.

These books were powerful! I say that because anything you read that leads you to become the protagonist, engaging in those same actions, is dangerous. I wanted out of my life, only to live out this fantasy. Although I wasn't bold enough to do the things I read, I wanted to. That's all the devil needs is a workshop in your mind. I couldn't wait for those kids to do independent work, just so I could sit and read. I know I pissed off my co-worker.

She told me one day, "All you want to do, Ms. Mitchell, is tend to the children and read your books. I never know what is wrong with you. You don't talk to me."

She was right. She was a young white woman who could barely control her class without my intervention. I started resenting the fact that, here I was, older than she was, but her assistant. I was only called upon to *control* the class.

I was *THE HELP*.

Honestly, if I wanted to, I could have finished school with my bachelor's and taught my own class, but that wasn't what I wanted to do. I was good at it. It just wasn't my desire. So, I settled.

I found a new escape in my life through these intense stories. I went from reading one book to five. Then, from five books to ten. It was some kind of obsession. I would sit in class, and between my legs would get so wet that I would need to go to the restroom. I was horny as hell, and I loved it! I walked around with a huge smile on my face.

Until one day, those stories became my own. There were a few women at the job who also enjoyed a good read. Some didn't read at all because they just enjoyed partying. It was someone's bright idea that we go and *GET SOME MONEY!* I'm not talking about robbing any banks or anything like that. I'm talking about escorting. That's just a fancy way of saying prostitution. My friend came to me and told me that she and a few other teachers' assistants were sick of the $12 per hour job we had. They wanted to use what they had in order to get what they wanted. The plan they wanted me to be a part of was this...

We would buy wigs, go out of town to some bars, pick up men, name our price, and *SCREW THEM*. They literally had meetings on how to get started. They were serious and wanted me to be a part of it. Crazy enough, those books I had been reading gave me just enough courage to try. I would start to imagine how it would be. We were going to get paid, alright. I couldn't believe I was really in agreement with being an escort. For God's sake, I was raising a toddler, I was pregnant a few months before that, and now I was digging myself into a deeper hole.

What in the hell was wrong with me?

I was hurting. I didn't know what to do with my pain, so I suppressed it. I drank away my pain at times, and when I had a boyfriend, I let him screw it out of me. Long story short, my soul was dying.

Around this same time, I was going out every weekend, and one day after work, I pushed up on this engineer hanging from a light pole. He was working for the electric company. My co-worker and I, who was much older than me, went to the bank. That's around the area where I met this fine yellow man. His body was tight and right. He had nothing but muscle. He was all of that. We spoke briefly as we sat at the light. I pulled off, but as I looked in the rearview mirror, he waved his hand for me to come back. So, as I laughed, I circled the block. This time we exchanged numbers.

After we talked for about three weeks, we met up and *OH MY GOODNESS!* This man, who was a little older than I, put his thang on me. I was intimate with him. So much so, I would laugh as he screwed me. He did the craziest and strangest stuff. He was amusing to me, but I never caught feelings for him. He was very cute, but because of the things we did, I knew it wouldn't go further than that. I was now training my mind to cut off any kind of emotional attachment. All he was... was a good lay.

A funny lay.

One night, my friend and I went to a club where he was working as a bouncer. He had some fine friends. Funny enough, he himself inquired about my friend. He wanted us to come over to his house later. I asked him if he wanted my friend. He said he wanted us both. That night, we didn't go to his place.

A few nights later, I brought her over to his place. I would not let him touch me. It turned him on all the more. I decided to watch him screw her, and that alone turned me on. After that, any time he wanted to see me, I refused. All of a sudden, I was turned off.

Was this what it felt like when a man deals with a "fast girl?" They no longer have respect for her?

That was exactly how I felt when it came to him. He could never get my heart or any kind of affection. This was the first man I had ever dealt with that I thought this way about. I never even had casual sex with anyone I didn't care about. My goal was always to be in a relationship.

At this point, I was only doing me. A few months later, everything changed. This very same guy, who I wasn't even seeing anymore, invited me over to a hotel party. He told me to bring about five girls with me. I only brought three. Boy oh boy, was I in for a night! This night would be the first and last night I would ever engage in this kind of activity.

I really didn't understand what was taking place. I walked straight into a sex party! It started as conversations with everyone. Then, slowly but surely, people broke up into groups. They were smoking and drinking. I didn't smoke, so I had something to drink. My company smoked weed with some of the other people. I remember being in a group and sitting on the couch with my male friend. He began to have a discussion about how it felt to have sex with us all individually. I looked around in shock at the fact that this man was literally talking about his sexual encounters with us. Then, I realized I was one of many. I didn't feel special at all. We were all his **WHORES!**

It definitely wasn't a good feeling. I was not flattered by far. I actually felt gross. When he began to talk about our experiences, I held my breath.

He said, "Fucking Angie made me feel like we was making love. Yea, she got some good sex. Real good."

I swallowed my saliva hard. All of a sudden, his description of me made me feel like a **TOP WHORE!** That's right! I was good, and probably unforgettable... unforgettable until his next dose of whores.

Oh my goodness, that was gross to be in a setting like that. Nothing to be proud of.

... The crap people do in their twenties...

Desperately, I wish I could forget. I would slice my daughter's eyeballs open if I knew she engaged in any of this evil, demonic crap! I literally would peel back her brain and pour anointing oil inside of it! I'm not kidding.

Anyway, I went to the back room, and this brown-skinned man, who was cute but not like my friend, started a conversation with me that eventually led us to the bathroom. When we walked inside, I asked him why we were there. He told me he wanted some privacy. He said he wanted me all to himself. I was confused because I only wanted to talk. He started kissing me on the neck. I told him we should go back out. He told me that I would be ok there with him because he didn't want people in his business. I told him that I thought that was the point for everyone to chill with one another. He ignored what I said and pulled me in close to him. He pulled down his pants and pulled out the smallest penis known to mankind.

Where did he think that thing was going?

Now, I understood why he wanted to be *ALONE*. It was a laughable sight to see! So, I told him that I was not having sex with him in the bathroom.

He said, "Come on."

Then, my male friend, let's call him Rah, busted through the door. He said, "Nah man, we don't do no closed doors in here. Why are y'all in here?"

The small, packaged guy said, " I wanted to be alone with her."

Rah said, " You at the wrong party partner. This ain't your girl, this my girl. Come on," he told me.

I followed him out like a lost puppy. That guy walked away looking sad. He would just have to find someone else who would accept that thing. Rah told me to wait on the bed and that he would be back. Now, this was just a hotel suite, so it wasn't that big. It only had a huge living room and a huge bedroom. In the bedroom where I was, there were about 5 or 6 other people. My friend who came with me and my cousin were entertaining two other men. My friend was putting a condom on someone's private parts and began sucking it.

I couldn't believe my eyes! Then, he bragged about how good her head was, even though he wore a condom. So, the other guy couldn't wait for his turn. She sucked him off just like a soldier. It was hilarious! Then, one of them started having sex with her from the back while she kept giving the other guy head. I was drunk as hell; however, I remember that like it was yesterday. I just couldn't believe I was witnessing this porn-like activity in real time. I remember thinking, *This has got to be a dream.*

Oh, it gets better! Then, Rah came back into the room with a female. He laid me on the bed and started to kiss me. I like that part. In my head, I was thinking, *I know we are not about to have sex with a room full of people?* Then, he undressed me, and held my arms back, while this natural curly-haired skinny black girl performed oral sex on me. Not only did I laugh, but I told her to stop.

I was like, " I'm drunk, I'm not gay! What are you doing?"

She said, "I know what you like. I'm gonna eat you better than any man."

I beg to differ. I didn't make any sounds. My friend asked me if I liked it. I told him it felt weird. Then, he stopped her, and he took over.

Now, that feels amazing!

I don't know what the hell she was doing. It was stopped by my cousin walking in and pulling me up from under him.

You see, what happened was, she was headed to the bathroom, and saw my purse open with my wallet out just lying there. My other friend also stopped screwing those guys. It seems like everyone came into that room at that moment. I put my clothes back on and looked through my purse for my debit card. It was gone!

I panicked.

I asked the other girls in the room and in the living room to show me their pocketbooks. They blacked out and made up stories about why they wouldn't take my money, and some of those girls were snobby as hell. I was trying to explain to them how. I explained, if the shoe were on the other foot, they would look for their stuff, too. They weren't hearing me at all. So, my cousin and my coworker took out their phones and told me to cancel my card. My coworker had Bank of America on speed dial. Somehow, I remembered my account number, even though I was drunk, and I canceled the card.

In 3 years, I had never gotten my taxes back when I filed. This was the first time I received $4000 back in taxes. It came through the day before this wack ass party, and I was on the verge of losing it all!

Thankfully, my account wasn't touched at all... at least not yet. My friend and cousin had stopped it before it came to that. The

Lord truly knew I may have killed myself had they cleaned out my account.

In the midst of that madness and total filth, God had shown mercy on me. This buffed-out-looking white guy was hanging around my bag, and I asked him as well. Of course, he cried the blues. Then, my so-called male friend Rah came into the room and told me how dare I accuse his friends. He said that the white boy had more money than my entire family. The freaking nerve of him! At that point, I was on my way to slap the hell out of him when my cousin and friend pulled me out of there and said, "Let's go, we are leaving now!"

SO I WALKED OUT TALKING MASSIVE SMACK!

I couldn't believe he was covering for his slutty friends. My cousin drove my friend home, and we went back to my cousin's home drunk. I believe I spent the night with my cousin. That next morning, I checked my account again... all of my money was still there. I was extremely grateful. There were no words to describe what I felt, but I will make an attempt.

I felt dirty.

As I drove home to get my baby from my mother, I started to REPENT TO GOD.

I felt NAKED!
I FELT NAKED!
I WAS NAKED!

MY SIN HAD BEEN EXPOSED! GOD SAW IT ALL! HE SAW EVERYTHING I DID! I WAS GUILTY AS CHARGED! THROW THE BOOK AT ME! THROW EVERYTHING AT ME BECAUSE I WAS BUSTED! I WAS FULL OF SHAME! I deserved the penalty of death! The devil was clearly my master, and there was no reason for god to show me any mercy!

However...he showed mercy by the TONS. With his loving kindness, he drew me back to him. I was in the car, screaming! I was crying! I tried my best to cover up my already fully clothed body, but it was ineffective!

I was still naked!

My sin had found me out and brought me into CONDEMNATION! I was in the dark, for real. Now, God's light and his kindness were impressed upon my heart. I felt his tender mercy, and I didn't understand why. *Why did he spare a sinner like me?* I wasn't thinking about him. I was thinking about my pain. I surely wasn't trying to obey him.

According to how I felt, I blamed him for a lot of my pain. I was caught red-handed, and God did not judge me. Instead, he loved me. Whatever his charge was, it would have been in his righteous judgment. I would have accepted it all. I did not care about myself. This was the lowest I had ever stooped. I understand sin is sin. Not to me, though. Some things were downright nasty. Some things were downright degrading. I was part of that club. Someone who was raised in the church was caught up doing the nastiest, worldliness, and most carnalest things!

I disgusted myself!

The memories of these personal encounters make me sick to my stomach. To relive this and write it down is shameful. I realize there is one judge who could have and should have destroyed me.

So, I beg you... yes, you...

Who thinks it could never be you? I beg you, never let it be.

Keep God at the center of your life.

Keep forgiving people who have hurt you.

Keep praying.

Keep carrying your cross and walk out your salvation with fear and trembling.

Don't for a second listen to the lies that the enemy has to tell you. The moment you do, you forget who you are and what you look like.

That day as I cried in the car, I felt God's forgiveness. I cried out, "Lord, save my soul! Please don't allow the enemy to kill me! I can't believe what I have done! Lord Jesus, save me, please!"

He did just that. There wasn't enough water in the shower to cleanse away my sins. I decided to fall to my knees and allow God to make me whole again and to grace me with his presence once again. *Whatever you do Lord, please don't take your spirit away from me,* I thought to myself.

As the days went on, I sought out the Lord. A week into work, my coworkers noticed a change within me. They didn't know it had anything to do with dedicating my life back to the Lord. I really didn't care what they thought.

I threw away most of my provocative reading material. The other ones, I gave to a few people, including the security guard. When my friend addressed me about being ready for the escorting job we were in the process of setting up, I told her I had started going back to church and was no longer interested in that. Not to mention, I was never as confident in it as they were. I knew I would chicken out. I don't think I would've ever gone through it. Then again, *does any prostitute plan to live that life?* They take drugs just to numb their reality of what they are doing. I'm sure it can't be easy.

Never say never!

Pray to God that he will keep you from the evil that the enemy will constantly present you with. No one is exempt! Without God, we will fail.

PERIOD!

One thing I'm sure of is that with sin, you don't have to look for it. When you are living apart from the will of God, sin finds you, MULTIPLIED! I didn't look for or plan to do any of those things I did. It wasn't in my heart to do all that crazy stuff. My motive was never to hurt other people or to live recklessly. However, when you're not submitted to God, you don't have a say-so. You can't say, " Oh, I'm gonna play with a little bit of sin."

What happens is, you get in too deep over your head. Then, you lose your will and continue to fall into temptation. You continue because it feels good to the flesh, and at the same time, it numbs you from reality. Most things I got into, I didn't even realize I was being set up... set up by the enemy! I wasn't in agreement with any of it, but somehow I went with it to avoid shame or embarrassment. I wanted to be part of something different or special. I did not enjoy my life. I did not enjoy being me. I wanted to inherit another life.

God just wasn't moving fast enough with the change. So when I attempted to change it without him, the devil was the one to pick it up and direct the course of my life. A life not submitted to God will always attract the attention of the enemy. We already know you can't serve two masters. I had to break, repent, and humble myself before the Lord, ask for forgiveness, and allow him to restart my life again. Any man who is in Christ becomes a new creation. Old things are passed away, and behold, all things are made new. Be made new in Jesus Name!

CHAPTER ELEVEN: THE MOVE

I'M OUT!

I planned to move down south to North Carolina after school ended, and that is exactly what I did. I met this big-time drug dealer named Junior. Well, I found out that truth later on. We met at this popular breakfast spot in a town across from where I resided. I was on my way to see my ex-boyfriend's mother, who was in rehab recovering from cancer. She wanted a toasted bun with Taylor Ham, and I was going to give her just that. I only had five dollars to my name, so I was praying to God that the sandwich wouldn't run me over. So, that was when I walked up to the door, and this fine, tall, semi-chocolate brother called me out from his car. We spoke briefly. He told me he was in his work car and was picking up food for his workers. Back then, we called old-looking, outdated-looking cars, HOOPTIES.

He had to clear up the fact that the car wasn't up to par, according to his cat pulling, pimped out style of luring women in. If he had it his way, he would have pulled up in his Porsche or one of his other expensive cars when he met me in order to prove he had money... as if he could buy me. This shows you how he was used to attracting women because of his wealth. Wealth created legally and illegally.

"Sir, I am not interested."

He said, "Interested in what? I just want to see that beautiful smile again."

Of course, my silly behind cracked a huge smile. Then, he opened the door for me. I placed my order, and when it came time to pay for it, he asked me if that was all I was getting.

I replied, "Ummm, yea."

He said, "Oh, ok then."

Then, I added an orange juice.

He smiled and paid for the food. I told him the food wasn't for me and told him where I was headed. He pulled out his phone and told me to put my number in it. He damn sure didn't ask. I was taken aback by his fast talking, boss-man confidence. I informed him that I was making plans to move myself and my 3-year-old to North Carolina in a matter of a month. He told me that it didn't matter because he had rental property out there, so he could see me when he wanted.

"Put your number in my phone", he said again.

I obeyed! Then, he told me that he would see me soon.

I saw him a few times that month. I only took a few rides with him while he was doing work stuff. He didn't give me any money, nor did we have sex. We only had conversations. Two weeks were left before I was planning to move. Junior asked me who was moving me. I didn't know, nor did I have the money. He told me that his boys would move me because they owed him a favor. I believe 'til this day that they must have transferred illegal goods in that truck. I can't imagine any other reason why a stranger would pay $1800 to move me, especially seeing as though I never slept with him.

I told him, in three weeks, I was coming back to Jersey to visit my family. When three weeks had passed, I was back in New Jersey. Not only did I visit my family, but I also met him at a hotel and got acquainted with him in a whole other way. He was well endowed. A little too much. He made me feel like an amateur. He enjoyed me, but also clowned me because I wasn't as comfortable and experienced as he expected, I guess. I still met him again before I left, for round two.

Unfortunately, everything with him was so rushed, as if it were business as usual. I didn't feel comfortable. We continued to meet, but not for sex. He just made time for me when he was in my town, and we only saw each other for 20 minutes. Then, I went back to North Carolina. He never came to North Carolina to see me. It didn't matter because I was back in New Jersey every three months, for a year.

The woman I bought the sandwich for, eventually died from cancer. I was devastated! I saw Junior again around that time. For months on end, I wouldn't hear from him. Eventually, he fell off, and I had several different relationships in between. Strangely enough, my brothers would bump into him and tell him I was in town.

After my awful separation from my then-husband, I moved back to New Jersey. That was something I never intended to do. EVER!

I never saw Junior as my man. We were friends. Besides the money from the move, I never asked him for anything, and he never gave me anything. He ended up in prison for 9 years. I visited him for a few years off and on, even when I was in my long-term relationship. I totally disrespected my man at the time. However, my friendship with Junior was also important. We wrote too many letters to count. When he got out in 2014-2015, I picked him up from the train station that same week. I never met his family, friends, or anything. He revealed to me through letters that he was married and had divorced his wife. All that time we were friends, and I never knew that.

I had an emotional connection with a married man.

I had a soul tie with a married man.

A man who made one thousand promises to me about things he would do for me if I wrote him letters and went to see him. If I received his calls and waited for him, he promised to take care of my every need. We know how that story goes because when they get out, you become a vague memory. That was the last time I saw him, and we only had two conversations afterwards. That man was connected to me in a different way. For years, I had hoped to see him changed, free, and delivered. I spoke to him so much about God and having a relationship with him. I wanted him to join me in church, as he promised he would. Life isn't perfect, and we are not without sin. I just didn't want him to live a lifestyle that could end his life prematurely. I was trying to save him. I pray that seed was sown and that God led him unto himself.

By this time, back in North Carolina, I lived a quiet life. A life away from my family and most of my friends. I had a boyfriend, who eventually wanted to marry me, but I ended that on account that he wasn't a Christian... which eventually led us to doing things that weren't expected of me. I was tired of it. He also cheated when we were apart for two days, and then reconnected. He drank a lot at that time. He was a good countryman and nothing like the bad-boy urban men I dated. He enjoyed family life. I was in the pursuit of holiness. We definitely were unequally yoked. I was really seeking God, which led me to not be interested in him any longer.

When I left North Carolina and moved to Alabama to do full-time ministry, I became involved with my ex-husband. When he found out, he was devastated. He couldn't believe how I got married so fast. Til this day, I not only regret that mess of a marriage, but I also don't understand the point of it. Some people believe that in life, you should never have regrets because those things teach you a lesson. I learned a lot, absolutely. However, to understand the significance of something is another story. I wasn't even attracted to the guy. It was his love for God that was more attractive. In the world, he would have been the last person I looked at. We also had nothing in common. I wanted to be a wife, and he claimed to want to be a good husband. Neither one of us stuck around to see that happen.

After I moved back to New Jersey, I was happy to be surrounded by family and friends who had my back, especially my family in the body of Christ. I was being restored. I dated a few people and even got engaged. That engagement ended because I was with someone with whom I had a history with, but no longer had a connection. He was a friend of my brother, whom I first dated when I was 20 years old. We dated for a year or so and broke up. However, we remained friends. We tried every few years to date again, but it never worked out. So, when I came back to New Jersey, he jumped on the bandwagon to try to marry me.

Before I left New Jersey to move to North Carolina, I wanted to be with him, even as friends, but he didn't want to leave his job as a fireman to come start a life with me out there. He would have had to take a pay cut. So, he let me go. However, before I got divorced and before I dated Mr. A. We reunited, dated for some months, got engaged, and then separated again. We fought like cats and dogs. I began dating someone at church, whom I actually started seeing while I was engaged. He was one of the reasons why I gave the ring back to my ex-fiancé... we will call this man Mark.

We got really close, so much so that I cut my fiancé off completely. So much for doing that, because I found Mark to be a control freak and a cheater. He was extremely spoiled and self-centered. Everything had to be about him. So because of the issues we were having, we grew apart. He found out about my new friend, Mr. A, and asked me to leave him alone to give us another chance. However, that was only after I found out about him and someone at his job, whom he took to the beach. They were definitely close. He found her to be very attractive. He spoke of this woman a few times during our relationship.

One day, he was trying to show a friend of ours a picture, and I asked to see it. I didn't stop at the picture. I continued swiping to the right, and behold, there were pictures of him and her, cuddled up on the beach when he should have been at work. He snatched his phone from me. I was heated, but played it off as if I were cool. I told him not to even worry about it. He lied, of course, and said it was nothing. He explained to me that we were not getting along recently and that he had made a mistake taking her out. He told me that it was over between them. That was when I told him about Mr. A and how he was bringing lunch to me at work. Up until that point, I never went out with Mr. A. I just had personal conversations with him, and allowed him to treat me special, but I never kissed him, and we were never physical.

Of course, Mark was upset to hear that story. However, his response shocked me. He told me that we had both gotten other people out of our systems, and that we could start afresh... like nothing ever happened. All we had to do was move on from there and not look back. We had this conversation on my friend's swinging canopy in her backyard. Again, I acted as if I didn't care and smiled. I couldn't wait to leave Mark's sight after that so I could tell Mr. A what just happened.

It wasn't all about receiving things from Mr. A.... he was easy to talk to. He was a teddy bear. So, I decided to go and continue my relationship with Mr. A. I was happy. Mr. A treated me better than any man had. He really knew what it was to be a grown man. He knew the responsibility involved in having a girlfriend, and I didn't need to ask him or tell him anything. He understood the assignment, and I fell deep in love.

As time went on, my actions of catering to Mark went down one hundred percent. I stopped washing his clothes, cooking for him, going out with him, and spending the night. I was over him. He noticed and started to call me more. He began accusing me of cheating. One day, he called me when I was with Mr. A. I was so nervous because I had never spent the night out with Mr. A, and Mark just kept calling. He called me and told me that he felt like something was off. I continued to deny it and lie about being out with my friends. I said I was coming home, but never called him. He blew my phone up all night long. He let me know he knew I was lying. I assured him that I was going home. Then, I turned my phone off.

Mr. A brought me home by 6 AM, and Mark was at my door by 6:45 AM. I was so nervous. Mark continued to tell me how terrible he felt all night, and how his spirit was telling him something different. We were only calling each other out of obligation, and not out of love. We were not in love anymore. Finally, I was in the open with Mr. A, and out of the blue, Mark came back around trying to convince me to give him another chance. He told me that it wasn't fair that I was letting this new, older man, who was experienced, come tear us apart. He said that we could grow together and learn what works for each other, that Mr. A had already had his experiences with being married before and having children, and that I needed to give us a chance.

I told him some things can't be undone. The lies and cheating were too much, and I had already given too much to this man. Now, I was with Mr. A, and it was too late. I was not going to stop seeing him, and that was what I told him. He drove off, upset, and started bashing me to people in church. He was very evil and disrespectful. Eventually, he moved away and lived his life seeking others to fill his void.

For the first time, I felt safe with this man. He was 40 years old when we met. I was 30 years old. One day, when I was working at Wilsons Leather, a leather retail store, Mr. A walked in with his uniform on. He had a nicely built upper body and had salt and pepper hair. He thought he was younger, so his choice of a hairstyle was pretty juvenile. He wore cornrows going back. I admit, he had a little swag. I didn't know at the time that he was checking me out as well. I approached him and asked him if he needed any assistance, and he told me he did. He asked me my opinion on a leather handbag. I asked him who it was for, and he told me it was for his daughter.

So, we picked out a bag together. I still remember... it was a tan, all-leather handbag. I rang him up and he thanked me. He had this deep voice and a sexy smile. He knew exactly what he was trying to do. I saw him before, walking past the store and looking in, but I never had the honor of helping him with a purchase. About thirty minutes after he left the store, his friend dropped off the same bag that I had rang up and told me I could have it. I refused to take it. However, the guy left and left me the bag. I remember that I had to explain to my boss what happened, or I could have gotten fired.

The next day or two, Mr. A came back to the store, and we began to talk. I complained about the guy I was dating at the time, and he gave me advice. Part of that advice was going out with him, which I did later on down the line. At this point, I knew my relationship was over with my ex. I was no longer interested in doing for a man who clearly wasn't giving me his all. I was over him, and in my heart, I moved on to Mr. A. He started asking me what I wanted for lunch and made sure I received it. He began to spoil me from the first time we met. That wasn't the reason I loved him, though. He was patient, kind, giving, handsome, friendly, and very aware of what he wanted.

For sure, a man like this couldn't be single, right?

Right. He was still married, but separated for over ten years. Even in his separation, he had another 13-year relationship that he had ended. He told me he had been working on a divorce, but because of the kids, he couldn't. He needed them to be a little older.

Unfortunately, he relayed this information a couple of months in, when we were already getting close. It took him four months to blow my entire mind... might I add, blow my body out. I had never been with a man who was that experienced. This guy intentionally tried to ruin my mind and my body. I was open like the Red Sea. We did everything together. He never brought his drama home to me. Eventually, I let him meet my daughter and my mother. Until this day, they love him.

Unfortunately, after years of dating and him not allowing me to have a relationship with his children because of their mother, I grew tired. After he still hadn't made a decision to divorce, even though for over ten years neither one of them was living together and both were in other relationships, I started dating other people. He made me believe we would marry, but because of money issues and fear that his ex would get half of his pension, he never divorced her. I was so tired of the excuses. After four years, I started dating again.

I remember when my daughter was between 10 and 11 years old, and she walked me outside to speak these words, "Mommy, I'm tired of seeing you cry. Mr. A will never marry you. I know you want to get married and you love him, but he will never marry you."

I gave her a hug, and told her what she was seeing was correct. I said to her, "I know, Chunka, I know. That's why I'm moving on."

Mr. A and I continued to break up and get back together for a short time, but even that got old. He still wasn't ready to end his old life, so we could begin. He started to go back to his old ways and dated multiple women. They were 20 years younger than he was. He also began drinking heavily. He claimed to never love them, but you know, he told them whatever he had to in order to continue getting what he wanted. My family adored him, and so did I. Years passed, and we finally broke up. At the mention of his name, while in my other relationships, they envied Mr. A, and they all had the right to.

My ex, Mark, came back into town to live and started to pursue me. He also came back to the same church we attended. This time, I was going to play it safe and take things slow. I entertained it for a while, and even went on a date with him. I listened to him tell me how he never stopped thinking about me, and how he wanted to make me his wife. He wanted to make my daughter his stepdaughter. I wore a ring that I received from Mr. A. It was given to me as a symbol that he would always be in my life. It wasn't an engagement ring. It was a promise ring. Mark asked me what I was going to do with the ring when we made it official. Mark also understood that I didn't want to just jump into a relationship with him on account of how it ended a couple of years before. I told him, if we dated again, I would keep the ring until we got married, and then give it to my daughter because she still had a relationship with him.

Who was really getting rid of a diamond ring?
Not me.

So, he understood... or at least made me think it was ok.

The next week, we got into a disagreement, and both backed off. However, he already asked me to go to the church banquet with him, and I agreed. I really just wanted him to pay for my ticket. I had already decided in my mind that he was going to work to be with me this time. When we dated before, I gave him all of me, much too fast. I learned a hard lesson because all he did was tell his friends about my goods... sexually, and all the perks he gained from being my man.

As that was happening, he decided to date my then-friend. As she was in my ear trying to convince me that he really loved me, she was also in his other ear telling him the secrets I swore that I wouldn't share about his business. However, if one friend shares a secret, then the other feels pressed to do the same. Boy, did I fall for it. My very own sister told me not to trust her, and was worried that we were spending too much time together. Her true colors were revealed when I asked the Lord to show me what was happening.

Ask and you shall receive. The Lord exposed it all.

The story was messy and involved a lot of church folks. I felt betrayed on a whole other level. They eventually dated and got married. My friendship with her meant more to me than that loser, but clearly, she couldn't be trusted either. I counted my losses and left the church I loved. It was no longer a place where I had peace. This was how I realized what was going on.

She and I were friends and did many things together. I spent time with her family and also had my daughter around her. We both headed ministries in the church. We were working out together on a daily basis, but this decreased. She would tell me stories about her and her involvement with her ex-boyfriend, so we compared stories, which is something friends do. However, she was using my stories to build her case. I don't know when it happened, but somehow it did.

She started to become more and more distant from me. She started making excuses not to come with me to work out or do other things. Then, she started posting stuff on social media showing off these gifts she was receiving from this secret man of hers. A man who was also a mystery to me. What was sad was that mutual friends of ours knew what was going on, but no one told me anything. Remember, we all attend the same church. I was beyond hurt. So one day, I asked her out with me and she agreed. She met me and Mr. A, who was still my friend, but nothing more than that. We went to eat lunch, and she finally met him. She told me he was handsome, but she didn't talk at all about Mark, like she normally would.

When we left to go to Walmart, I told her that when she gets a man that she will act like she didn't know me anymore. She stated to me that she wasn't that kind of person. I told her that I felt like she was hiding something from me. She denied it. I decided to stop asking her to work out with me because it began with me supporting her weight loss journey... but now, she was acting weird.

On Christmas morning, I cried out to the Lord to reveal what was really going on, and he did just that. I received a phone call that she was having dinner with family, and Mark was there. They said she was all in his face, making him plates of food, and serving him like he was her man. Eventually, she heard I kept calling her cousins, friends, and others looking for her because she refused my calls. She finally answered me with the nastiest attitude I had ever heard from her. She was bold and nasty, and told me that it didn't matter because I didn't want him. She was driving his new car, going places, and everything. This girl, who called herself my sister in Christ, had picked up my sloppy seconds and had the nerve to be upset at me.

We continued to argue, and I must have called her one hundred different names. I hung up the phone and cried for days. I was betrayed, hurt, and shamed when I did nothing. She wasn't even sorry! She was bold and nasty. She said all those things to me in front of him, but several days later, she left Facebook messages and begged me to speak with her. She also said she was sorry. I went to church, and everyone was staring at me. I could tell that they knew. The story was even in other churches. I heard all kinds of things about how he chose someone fat over someone like me... and worse. That didn't matter to me because it wasn't about size, although he was openly against dating heavier women. I didn't care about that. I couldn't

understand what I did to her to cause her to bring such pain to me. Some people just want what you have because they think it's better...
That is the furthest from the truth.
    I kept silent through it all, except for some trusted people I shared my feelings with. I didn't want to talk to anyone. Because of that situation, I walked away from a lot of people I liked, and some of whom I loved. Even my leaders were aware and advised her to tell me the truth. I don't blame them for doing what they thought was right, and even for marrying them. They were against it and did not find them to be compatible. However, you can lead horses to the water but can't make them drink.
    I needed to think about myself and my daughter. We attended the church for as long as we could. I even forgave them. After they got engaged, she came to me in a room in the back of the church and begged my forgiveness with an engagement ring on her finger. At that time, I did not forgive. It may have taken me years. I just knew that I had to leave the church that I loved. It was a painful transition. I couldn't be healed in a place that felt like pure betrayal. So, I moved on. It also affected my friends and family, specifically my daughter, who dealt with people treating her like she had done something wrong. However, my mother stayed.

My Truth, My Story

At the end of it all, I have learned that I may not own a lot of things, but my honesty is my truth.
It's one of the most important things I own.
It's all mine!
I claim it!
I live it!
It belongs to me.
People want to criticize you for speaking your truth.
The mess and all. The hypocrisy at times.
The hurt and the pain. The downfalls and the gains.
I own it all.
The praise, the glory.
In the end, it remains my story.
I won't be ashamed.
I'm not afraid of the claims.
My secrets, my diaries.
I'm sharing because it's all inspiring.
Not to encourage you to do all that I have, but to see through

my eyes of who I was back then.
Who I grew to be today.
Lost at times. Empty then full.
The journey has been long, and it continues to grow.
I'm sharing, all because I know.
Life isn't easy.
Life isn't fair.
But it's a journey that we all have to share.
What we do in this life has meaning.
It matters to us all.
And the way we live here today determines where we will go tomorrow.
There is a place to go after this all ends.
I hope you will take inventory of your decisions and somehow make amends.
For the good, for the bad, for the happy moments, and for the sad.
We are accountable for what we do.
And me? ...
I'm just crazy enough to share those times with you.

Where do I go from here? I never imagined what a father's love would do to me or the lack thereof. How it shapes in a lot of ways who you will turn out to be.

We say, "Let the girls be with the mother and let the boys stay with their dads."

Both are needed to ensure she always has. A daughter needs protection. A daughter needs love. She needs security. She needs to be nurtured. This was never a job for one parent, but for both. What ends up happening is that one parent tries to compensate for the absence of the other. Something will always be missing.

There are tools that are needed that a father must teach his daughter. If he doesn't, she will be at risk of falling for anything. Not only that, but she travels the world unprepared. Yes, I had three brothers, but it wasn't their job to instill those things. I'm sure they lacked love in more ways than I can count. Here are some things that two of my brothers remember about my father. They would like to share their stories. This is from my brother Nat, who is just eighteen months older than me. He is known as the baby boy, the last son my mother and father had.

CHAPTER TWELVE: MY BROTHERS

NATS WORDS AND MEMORIES:

As the youngest son of Erving Lee Mitchell, I expected to be spoiled, but not damaged. Howbeit, damage is another word for being spoiled. I became damaged goods, but wasn't spoiled! Well, at least not spoiled like most white kids, or as some fortunate black kids at the time.

My Dad had two other sons, but I couldn't tell you if he had any favorites. He was a good, godly man on the surface among relatives while with us. However, the carnal aspect of human nature perverted his sense of fatherhood. Perhaps that is just my observation decades later, being full of growing pains.

According to Uncle John, my father had gone from a "married godly man" to a "married ladies' man." After Vietnam, family life, and the typical Christian challenges, Dad changed into another version of himself. Well, at least towards his children, he was angry and troubled. Again, this is according to my uncle, who really only stated that the effects of the experience of war and how it altered his mentality, but I know that other things shifted his focus as well.

Drunkenness is what I've seen as a youth, and my mother often would take his socks off as she fixed his legs into bed. I desired his attention as the youngest boy. I had two sisters, which one of whom came after me, so she was the youngest. She definitely needed attention because she was the baby girl. We had that sibling rivalry thing going on for years! We both still grew up with voids of fatherly embraces and masculine loving words that would teach us love. However, I did later learn that my father's father had left his wife, so my dad's manhood wasn't spiritually mature enough to complete our family circle.

This cycle continues today! Even having a dad, we boys still needed ideas of manliness to act like men, which we struggled with. The enemy would rather we be as he was, effeminate and the opposite of what God called us to be. My father showed us work-related things, family gatherings, and fishing! This all was important, but I think a bunch of chores, spankings, and silence left no room for bonding. We boys grew up without loving virtues towards each other, and so we sought after fun and games! We laughed over ill feelings of unexplained voids and bad moods.

Therefore, we never expressed love despite our mother expressing it to us. A father's covering is obviously different from a mother's covering. He needed to be submitted to God so that his wife and children would have an example to follow. Women are not built to lead households. The home must be sealed and sanctified with a godly man's spiritual leadership. This is why he can change the tones, temperatures, and atmospheres of rooms in the home. When Dad said, "Stop crying and go to bed!" That is what we would do after Mom tried with her soft voice to no avail.

Childhood bullying became a normal thing that often occurred. Dad never became our "Superman" in this dark world of ungodly people. Maybe he had thought that because we boys weren't familiar with war, our problems were trivial and not to be examined, but he would examine wounded soldiers as a military medic!

We children had many internal wounds that needed treatment as well. Nobody sees these spiritual complications but God. We knew "Superman" was white like Clark Kent and Santa Claus, among other "worldly role models." Personally, I began seeing Dad as a weak man because TV depictions of these "savior figures" displayed that Dad didn't have those powers.

Bullying, peer pressure, and my brother's closeness had moved me to rebel. As the youngest son, I didn't consider that my two brothers were here before me. I just knew I was here and wanted attention! Then, my kid sister was born, so the shadows of myself became a playground for wrong thoughts and actions!

Why would I burn my sister on her neck with a lit cigarette that I was too young to even smoke?

Why did I experiment with her body by holding her nose and pressing her belly inwards?

That is just two things I did that were particularly stupid, but I was troubled and missing fatherly discipline. A discipline that could have taught me to love myself more than all others under the same roof, being family. I did love my family, but certain childhood issues broke my spirit. From one neighborhood to the next, there was trouble.

I became confused over brotherly love after being jumped with my brother, but he wasn't the target! He just watched me being pounded on by a certain bully with his friends. Every other neighborhood knew about this particular guy because this bully became the "Master Bully" for half of my teenage years in grammar and middle school. Every young boy who rode the yellow bus had to watch him with his little brother and a few of their comrades jump people.

Long story short, I had an evil eye against my own brother because he'd fight me... but not with me against my bully. Daddy was to blame for this trauma because he was supposed to protect me from evil! He was supposed to make sure that big bro taught the middle bro and the middle bro taught the little bro skills to fight! My oldest brother was another victim of bullying, and we all have our own personal stories of running and escaping.

Big bro gave us all hope through weight training, and eventually, his muscles became large enough to change some guys' evil intentions. Troublemakers would change direction or think twice about bringing trouble our way, but the master bully still played! He would tell me, "I'm not scared of your big brother, get him!" I never got big bro because I knew that this master bully had another big guy who had others waiting for drama. Therefore, I never involved my brothers with folks from other hoods. I knew they wouldn't play fair anyway. However, if there were problems within our area, I would go get big bro!

Big bro had a few fights behind me and my middle brother. I suffered a bloody gash over my left eye trying to fight an experienced guy from the block named D Mac. He was the big bro to three younger brothers who became my friends later, but why did I feel the need to jump to the forefront while other friends were trying to fight D Mac? It's because I needed attention!!! Well, I surely got it after a blow that bloodied my face.

I had a white T-shirt over my head, dripping in blood! Everyone came to my aid, and I even fought the guy harder. Then, they started throwing sticks and rocks at D Mac. Later, my big bro had to fight him to prove his big brotherhood.

This is my story, and it cannot be recorded in its fullness, but know that I lived with a mental illness. It had fixed my mentality for decades, but only Christ within me had softened me up for compassion. Much of my aggression turned into forgiveness and kindness, but still today, "shit talking" only reminds me of past bullying.

Today, there are trigger words for probably all of us that could reignite old pains that could place us on edge, *but how could a father understand his children when he himself is troubled over the practical affairs of life?*

So, Dad wouldn't be able to tell me anything because of his lack of care and affection for my personal challenges. When I learned how to smoke and drink, it was my new secret. The same with sex, whether it was masturbation or fornication.

Who was going to school me about these life choices and carnal imperfections?

School teachers could never take our parents' role as being our first teachers. However, if they failed to teach us thoroughly about life challenges, then we would search elsewhere. Unfortunately, too many of us never got the answers we needed prior to experiencing situations.

However, our parents were blind to certain aspects as far as spiritual warfare. We couldn't expect them to know it all! I could say this now as an adult believer, "Free will and free choice is God's free gift, but without spiritual instructions, we are just targets for madness!" We know small trouble escalates into bigger trouble, but somebody's prayers sent angels after us all.

Mom always fellowshipped with prayer warriors within churches. I was always in somebody's heart, and if it wasn't Momma's heart then it was one of her friends in Christ. The question is, *why didn't my father do what my mother had done, sitting on my bedside, interceding hands on?* I just can't remember him doing that as Momma did it, but to God be the glory! I am grateful for every prayer, known and unknown, from both parents!

Many large families within our neighborhoods went from having five sons to two sons or seven daughters to four! Just calculate the reasons and statistics of what has destroyed our youth! Prayers have certainly kept my family from reaping what had been sown. Perhaps, we were undeserving of God's grace and mercy at times. The truth is that many of these families didn't have praying mothers and fathers. I hope someone is encouraged to stand in the gap for their children. Troubled souls have always found their way into the devil's playground.

It was too easy for me to physically fight my Dad when I hated myself. I was picked on as a dark-complexioned child all my childhood. Black was evil, according to the dictionary and according to the depictions on *white* TV. For this reason and others, I fought people and didn't care about being scarred for life. My skin was the greatest scar anyway, according to hikes, or jokes of peers, but more than this... heated arguments with family using the same loose words.

Words became weapons against me, and if the right person said something, it would hurt my soul! I loved my sisters always, but their words confirmed what everybody said against me. I loved my brothers, but their closeness made me feel disconnected. I'd find other troubled teens like myself to walk with for smiles, hugs, and laughter. At least laughter was good for my heart until some big head wanted to hike for hours! Once I'd run out of laughs, it was time to fight, and folks just couldn't understand my inner pains.

I was a loser in their eyes who couldn't take jokes, but they didn't know my secrets. I loved my Dad, but he never got inside my heart, and so I felt he was unworthy to bear my secrets. *He wasn't the best version of himself, so how could he help me?* Apparently, he was in some spiritual bondage that had kept him in a low state! I am my father in terms of spiritual battles and manhood. Therefore, if I could say, "I'm so sorry, Dad," I would with tears and snot pouring from my nose.

White privilege had helped me to hate myself as a child. Plus, I was sexually molested and wrestled with my sexual identity. Eventually, my childhood friends had become partners in trouble-making. I enjoyed being high on weed and being drunk from alcohol because it helped me to escape reality. Day by day, I'd look forward to escaping reality because Dad wasn't happy, and Mom was just functioning or pretending to be happy.

Any adult drama was nothing but noise to me, so if they'd fuss, I'd shake it off and continue playing. Now that I am older, I could praise their strength and will to maintain relations until Dad passed on. Yet, while he'd lived, the whole "Daddy" thing blew over my head. That longing for some type of Superman, fatherly relationship vanished as more sin captivated my mind. I became a troubled teen who loved nothing until God's word entered my heart.

When my Dad was discovered to be sick, I eventually softened up and attempted to be a better son. I suppose I was guilty of years of rebelliousness, but I was troubled early as a child. After believing in my heart that I could love my dad, he then passed away! All I remembered was a decent conversation we had while working in Uncle John's yard.

At the time, my heart said, "I could love Dad right this time." I had the idea of love and communication, but I waited too long to practice it. Sadly, these same...come too late... practices had carried over into our girlfriend and boyfriend relationships. Most times, we wait too long to repair things for the restoration of our minds. Peace of mind is everything because stress kills and creates physical diseases, which weigh heavily on the mind. No wonder many men don't take their girlfriends into marriage.

> **Proverbs 5:18-19**
> *Let thy fountain be blessed: and rejoice with the wife of thy youth.*
> *Let her be as the loving hind and pleasant roe; let her breasts satisfy thee at all times; and be thou ravished always with her love.*

If we men are corrupted by worldly people, places, and things, then our minds will continue to deviate from who and what God placed in front of us. Once this deviation takes root, the distractions, whether it be from alcohol, drugs, or others, will dominate our thought processes. Our minds warp through different channels of distractions and fantasies that are created within our hearts. Then, we draw further away from our girlfriends and family members.

Generational curses need to be broken by all means. It all boils down to us walking in God's love to spread love together over our sons, daughters, nephews, and nieces. Children must grow in spiritual love with honest communication, especially at dinner tables. Not one family member needs to be in another room on their cell phone or computer while everyone else is together. We must create *No Family Left Behind Rules.*

"A family that prays together, stays together."

This is a true saying.

For the countless souls who'd been without their father's love and covering, may The Heavenly Father bless you with a man who knows how to be a cover. Let him pay attention to your vulnerabilities and shared secrets, but let God into your crying hearts!

TYRONE'S WORDS AND MEMORIES:

While I'm actually grateful to have had a Father who stayed married for over 20 years, I know a lot of it was Mom's decision because of five children. However, his constant presence made a difference in my life, especially on 10 Alexander Street. He used to have a long, old Chevy 250 custom truck, and he just drove me around in it and *showed me off* to everyone. He used to say, "This is my oldest boy and he wants to be like me when he grows up."

When he affectionately pressed my body against his leg and showed me love, I was always overjoyed and felt a great sense of importance. He was right because I did want to be just like him... except for the drinking and smoking. Somehow, I got wisdom in regard to that part, but everything else I admired for the most part. Such as, I admired his great influence on others and the way he always helped people, constantly! Even when I didn't really understand it... I was always so curious. I used to peek out the window and see him giving money to people in the morning when he had gotten off work. He was a giver at heart, but so many people took advantage of him.

The times that he, Frank, and Fred, aka Sugar Bear, and I went freshwater fishing, those guys used to always ask Dad, aka Earp, for either money or beer. For the most part, it was given. We went on long fishing trips, and I also got to know his drunken, user, so-called friends.

Daddy was a damaged man as a result of the Vietnam War in 1968-1969. Every once in a while, I would ask him about his experience, and he looked at me, paused, looked away, and said, "I don't wanna talk about it." This used to leave me so frustrated, with so many unanswered questions, because I really wanted to know what happened during his year-long tour over there! This has still affected me today as I'm very much drawn to many war movies because I constantly thirst for answers.

GOD has been helping me in small doses. When relocating from Alexander St. to South Munn Ave in 1987, we embarked upon a new chapter. I was a skinny freshman at Westside High School, walking around nervously and not knowing what to expect. I used to always wonder where all this fear, doubt, and insecurity came from. The Holy Spirit revealed to me that it was passed down from my father... definitely a curse that still needs to be broken along with other curses in my life..

In 1988, I was a sophomore in high school. I came home one day and Mom had a meeting with us all and let us know that Dad was

HIV positive... *WOW!* All of our hearts dropped at the same time! This was the beginning of a lot of shame, disgust, embarrassment, anxiety, etc. Throughout the next seven years, he had to endure so much pain and shame. Everywhere I went, I had to hear, "Bro, what's wrong with your Father? Why is he so skinny?"

My way to pacify it was to say he was sick or that he was exposed to chemicals at his job. Whatever it took to keep the family secret and to get people the heck out of my face, I said. From year to year, I suffered mentally and emotionally, but it didn't stop me from being celibate... go figure! Shaking my head.

I learned from the years that we had a father who really loved the Lord, but had succumbed to his weakness and had to painfully and prematurely exit the earth at the young age of 49. I am now 49 and even with this void in my soul, I am still grateful for God's keeping power and I desire to break every generational curse of my life, in Jesus name!

I have a middle brother who I believe was affected greatly as a child and as an adult, but he doesn't choose to express those feelings. Whether he has forgiven my father or not is not known. He wants to leave his upbringing in the past. I pray one day he is able to share and be healed. Some things cannot be undone, so I do understand not wanting to revisit the past. I pray he has been restored. As for my other siblings, I am happy that they are connecting their pain to the past and forgiving my father for whatever he has done or did not do. They are brave for sharing their story. Now, I pray that they can move forward in peace, love, and happiness.

CHAPTER THIRTEEN: THE EMANCIPATION OF GIGI

It all started when I attended my cousin's church service in Alabama. I went to visit the new church they started, and that's where I met their godson. Now, at this time, I was still living in North Carolina. I was single because a guy that I had dated in NC had parted ways. Although I still cared for that man, I really wasn't interested in anyone else. I really was focusing on raising my daughter, who was four years old at the time. I was attending prayer meetings, bible studies, and church regularly.

When I went to my cousin's church, I was visiting for about a week. Their godson lived in the same town and became interested in me. We eventually exchanged numbers only because of my cousin's influence. He was brown-skinned, short, and wore his hair in a low cut. He was a little muscular, but that was only in his chest area. Later, I would find out how obsessed he really was about his weight. He was okay-looking compared to most of the people I've dated, but his clothing was bland. He didn't have any style, in my opinion. The only thing I enjoyed was his outward appearance of how he loved the Lord.

At this time, I was in the process of trying to break my lease so I could move to Alabama and start up a dance ministry at their church. My motivation to move from North Carolina to Alabama was strictly for the purposes of ministry, not for a man. However, a few months into talking on the phone with him, I grew to like him. When it was time for me to move, he and my youngest brother, Nat, were the ones who moved me. I was really happy to start over in a place where I thought would be my final destination. I really did not understand what was ahead of me.

Even in the beginning of a *thing*, it seemed to be the *end*. I could never get a break and just relax. It was always something that happened that catapulted my life into ruins. *Lord, when will it all end?* I was excited about my new life. I thought I was headed towards a life flowing with milk and honey. I thought that because I had sacrificed so much in my life, now had to be the time of fulfillment.

Of course, things were going well at first, but then we started not to get along. He appeared not to be happy about anything, and we disagreed about everything. Eventually, we stopped speaking with one another. My time with my cousins was cut short because my sister, back home in New Jersey, had an emergency. She was in need of a kidney, so I left Alabama to return to New Jersey to test if I was a match. My family was in great support of the transition. Needless to say, we were a match. I stayed with a family friend as the kidney donation took place. I stayed there for 3 months total. During that time, my ex and I spoke often and decided to make it work as boyfriend and girlfriend. So, when I returned, we resumed, and we got along better than when I left. He told me he wanted me to be his wife, but before he even told me, one day as we passed each other, I foresaw that I would marry him.

My cousins also agreed that it would be good for the church, seeing as though we were in a relationship. I agreed, but we still needed counseling... which we did not receive. It may have been twice that we sat down and spoke with our leaders. We planned to go to a beach in Florida in a month to have our wedding during a church event.

We never made it.

I had some issues with my cousin's husband because I ate out of his bowl. I wasn't aware of *his rules*. Even though I apologized and cleaned the bowl, it wasn't good enough. He even made comments about throwing me and my daughter out of the house and leaving our things on the steps outside. As I looked at him, I felt disrespected and insulted. So, I ran up the steps, packed my things, and called my boyfriend. I told him I was going to go back home to New Jersey. He came over, packed my things, and asked me to come stay with him. He knew I was against living with a man I was not married to, so that was when we decided, in the very next two days, to go get a marriage license.

Upon leaving the house and in the midst of packing all of my belongings, I ran into my cousin, who was coming up the stairs to check on me. We had a brief conversation about how she disagreed with the actions of her husband and that she would talk to him about it. I told her that I didn't expect her to defend me at all because I understood that she had to live with him. The last thing I wanted was to start a war between them. However, I didn't have to stay and take that. I had come all the way from North Carolina to start their dance ministry and also help build their new church in whichever way I could. So, what he said to me literally broke me down. Up until that very moment, I had submitted and respected his leadership, no matter how much I disagreed with his methods.

After I let my cousin know that I was leaving and that I didn't deserve that, she agreed and apologized on behalf of her husband. She assured me that she would deal with the issue in her own way. I'm sure she needed to use wisdom, and I never faulted her for not speaking up in my presence. I was always used to fighting my own battles anyway.

A few days after I had gone from their house, she let me know that she had said something to her husband. She did not argue with him, but she let him know how she felt about it, then she left it alone. Her opinion about it was that he was sorry. However, she told me that he would never apologize for it. She said I would pretty much see it with his actions. She definitely was right about my receiving no apology. His actions just appeared like nothing ever happened. Had it not been for that situation, I really don't believe we would have gotten married in such haste.

My sister gifted me with a beautiful wedding dress, and we made plans to go to Florida... nothing fancy. We decided to go to the courthouse only to get a license. It wasn't legal until my pastor signed it, so we went back to the church and announced it to my cousins. They were having a Bible study. Instead of us waiting like we wanted to wait, my pastor at the time, who was my cousin, wanted to have the commencement of the wedding. We had on regular street clothes, nothing even remotely dressy, and he married us. He also signed the license. We absolutely hated it, but my cousin told me that he wanted to have the honor of doing the ceremony first. This was the start of something horrible.

A week before it was time to prepare, my husband and I got into yet another argument and stopped talking. We made up shortly afterwards. Then I spent all my birthday money on him, trying to dress him and prepare him for the beach wedding... a wedding that never took place because, somehow, my cousins left without us. They thought we were not going anymore. 'Til this day, I never understood what happened or how communication was lost, so we just dealt with it. We still attended the church and worked in the ministry. My ex-husband was also ordained as a minister in the months to come.

Our marriage was so bad that I eventually moved out of the apartment I had moved into with him. I got my own place. I asked my cousin in New Jersey to send me some money to help me move and he did. After I moved out, I thought I could have a fresh start. However, we got back together, and he moved into my apartment this time. That joke of a marriage lasted only four months. I dealt with his cheating, bipolar attitude, self-hate, and jealousy. He would accuse me of even sleeping with the pastor, who is my cousin through marriage. He didn't like how I kept the house clean and cooked daily meals. He told me that I was too good for him and that my daughter and I should be with someone who could spoil us. He told me that all the meals I was cooking for him were making him fat. I agreed to go work out with him, and he only allowed it one time.

    He was emotionally abusive. He wouldn't talk to me most times, and when I tried to have sex with him daily, he usually rejected me and told me that he saw demons watching us, so he couldn't perform. Sleeping next to this man was a nightmare. I would feel like an elephant was sitting on my chest. I would cry to my cousins about what was happening, but nothing changed.

    I stayed crying. I was stressed out, losing weight, and I was already on the smaller side. I was no more than 115 pounds at the time. I did everything on my own. I did not have a job, even though I was trying to find one. I had only been recovering from the kidney donation surgery for 3 months. I still had yet to heal, yet this man showed no compassion. If it wasn't for Nat helping me out at that time, I don't know what I would have done. I was very confused as to what was happening in this marriage. I sought out wise counsel, but nothing helped. I grew more tired, depressed, and stressed, as he grew more jealous and miserable.

    When we were at church services and a guest preacher would call me out and prophesy, my ex-husband was never in agreement with it. He would always argue with me about what was spoken to me and then tell me that the pastor liked me as well. Something was really wrong with him. I was on a roller coaster. I prayed that God would deliver me, and this time, I would never go back.

    One day, he called me from his job and asked me to see if he had $10 in his wallet. He was on his way back home to pick it up. I looked through his wallet and found a picture of his ex. Of course, that was an argument. He didn't even have one of me and my daughter. I flipped out! I was so tired of the disrespect. Mind you, I am not a person who is short of words. I have a lot to say about everything. However, this man was another case.

    I clearly married the devil. I looked around for ways to do better... be better... dress better... cook better... perform sexually better, but this man wasn't interested in any of it. He made me feel like I was the crazy one. He even told me that the wedding ring I bought him didn't fit because we didn't fit as a couple.

One thing is right... we were terrible together.

I didn't deal with men like him on the streets, so why was I wasting my time now? I was trying to work it out because he was my husband this time, and not a boyfriend. One day, on the way to our friend's house, we were arguing about one of his disrespectful comments to me. When we got out of the car, I told him I would beat his punk ass. So, I picked up a long wooden stick that's used to build houses, I swung, and hit him twice.

He pulled it away from me. Our friends ran out to break us up. I stayed with my friend and slept on her cot for several days before I went back home. That was the first time he saw me in a rage, but it wouldn't be the last time. One day after Bible study, when I spent my last five dollars on food for him, he picked a fight with me. He asked me why I was always the one getting the good prophecies. I told him to ask the person who spoke into my life. The last spoken word into my life was that I would be able to take care of my family, and that God would supply all of my needs. That I would be alright. This preacher told me that God was going to bless me with so much that I could literally give my entire wardrobe away.

As I looked over to my ex-husband, his face looked like he had eaten sour grapes. So, when we got home, he started an argument. He went outside to his car to talk to some woman when we were supposed to be eating dinner together. It was Popeyes chicken. As I waited for him, time passed. So, I decided to creep up on him to listen, and he was in the process of telling some chick that he would see her soon over the summer in California, where he is from. I couldn't believe what I was hearing.

So, I reached my hand into the car and tried to bust his lip open. He bled just a little. I tried to snatch away his phone, but he managed to turn the phone off. He jumped out of the car and put me in a headlock. We looked all kinds of crazy fighting outside. He didn't hit me. He just restrained me. He started screaming out how he was from the "WEST COAST," and how I'm not to put my hands on him. I started laughing. I never saw him that angry. I told him to stop screaming and to go on with his punk self. I told him that he wasn't a minister, especially cheating on me. My pride was hurt more so because he let me spend my last five dollars on his broke behind.

Here I was, a 27-year-old with a 25-year-old. I never even liked younger men. I let this broke buster convince me that he was going to provide for me, love me, and take care of me like a real husband, and here we were playing house. I can't recall one thing he ever did for me. He never even purchased a wedding ring for me. I bought him his ring. When it was too loose, instead of getting it resized, he just kept twirling it around. Talking about some, " The ring doesn't fit because we don't fit."

There was a time he was even bleeding out of his penis because of some issue with having cobwebs inside his testicles. I convinced him to go to the doctors and have surgery. When he came back home, I went on a church trip to Texas that he couldn't attend. However, I left him three full-course meals at home. He didn't want for anything. Then, he realized that I was too good for him. So, he apologized for treating me badly. When I was in Texas, he admitted to saying crazy things to me so that I would leave him.

He admitted it!

When I think about it, this man said some really twisted and sad stuff to me. I didn't deserve any of it! Sometimes, I would just stare at him. No words spoken. I would just stare at him and wonder what I ever did to deserve a life with a sorry, dysfunctional man like him. I, too, was on the verge of going crazy from dealing with that mess. I was also too emotionally dysfunctional. So, I turned to God for help.

God gave me a dream that showed me him leaving with his bags. My stupid self turned over the next morning and told him about the dream. Then, he told me that he had a dream, too. He had a dream that I put him out. Funny enough, both were true because I packed up his bags and put them by the door. He walked inside the house, took his bags, dropped his keys, and took his grape Drink Ade beverage out of the refrigerator. That was the only thing he owned because everything else belonged to me.

I felt so free, light, and finally at peace. Until two weeks later. I felt like someone had died. I asked him over to the house to talk to me. He came over, and I begged him to stay. I even tried to have sex with him. It killed him that I packed his bags up, so he didn't forgive me. I cried, and he left.

My cousin came over to comfort me, and that was the first time I had a dream of angels comforting me. I wasn't in love with my ex-husband, but I feel like I did love him. I didn't like the idea of my marriage ending before it began. I never knew anyone to have a failed marriage in that time span. He would always say that people in his family never stayed married, so he was afraid. Yeah, I must agree. I gave it all I had, and at the end of it all, he wasn't worth my love or effort. It was the worst decision ever to marry him, but the best decision ever to get a divorce from him. I struggled with the fact that I thought God told me to marry him because he allowed me to see it. However, that is false.

Just because God showed you something, it doesn't mean he told you to do it. Those are two different things. My brother Nat was the one who gave me clarity on it. I was beating myself over a failed marriage; however, we can't change a man's will. He had great potential if he followed the ways of Christ. Thus, I refused to be in a marriage that made me feel less than. God has forgiven me, and life still continues.

I tried to stay in Alabama. I left my cousin's church and attended other churches. Nothing was the same. I did not receive the support there anymore. I needed my family. So two months later, my brother came to drive me and my daughter back to New Jersey with all of our things. A place I never wanted to move back to. It took us 17 hours to get home. We stayed one night in a motel. I was shamed and humiliated because I had failed in my eyes.

After months of being home, I heard life for him in California wasn't so sweet. We wrote some letters to each other. It sounded as if he was trying to reconcile. For a moment, I believed the same, but as time went on, it was clear we were not meant for each other. He told me he was no longer living as a minister. I knew exactly what that meant. I had dreams about his family, mainly his sister. I dreamt she died in a fire. One week later, she was hospitalized after being in a fire, and eventually died. I saw him revert to being a little boy again. I even saw him break his leg. I believe something like that happened, allegedly. He also started bleeding out of his penis again. I warned him that if he went back to that worldly lifestyle that his life would spiral and that his dick would bleed again. He admitted that part.

I asked him for half of the money for the divorce. He took forever just to give me $300. I decided to go ahead and file anyway. We didn't have any assets together, so it was pretty easy. In a few months, it was done, and my name was restored to my maiden name. I was so happy. By this time, I was in a relationship with Mr. A, and we had a "COMING OUT PARTY/COOKOUT". We called it "THE

EMANCIPATION OF GIGI!" Now, I was finally free to move on... and that, I most certainly did!

It took me years to understand what my part was in that horrible joke of a marriage. I had to take responsibility for my contributions. Yes, I did a lot of wonderful things. I felt like I was ready to become a wife. I felt like that because I was ready to do whatever it took to serve my family and build up the church, but I did not love my ex-husband in a way that prompted any couple to get married. I just figured I would grow to. Nor did I feel like he adored me in the way a husband should adore and honor his wife. We were willing to learn all of that, which was backwards. I got out of the will of God prematurely, because the spirit of offense was what ushered me into getting married.

Had we waited and attended relationship counseling first, I would have known the type of person he was and realized he wasn't what I wanted or needed. He was a wounded kitten looking for a mature woman to act as his mother. He had no sense of what it meant to provide and care for his family. He had no clue as to what that meant. As for me, I was still running from state to state, trying to create a new life with any man who was willing to continue to help me run. I was running from the control of my father and constantly into the arms of other controlling men. I ran from my cousin's house instead of waiting to be molded and shaped into a respectable wife. Yes, I do believe God already made me with those elements inside, and I already had the desire. However, I had a lot of baggage in my soul that brought additional trauma into my relationships. Instead of working through those problems, I just decided it was better to leave and replace them.

I'm not saying it was my fault that my cousin treated me in that manner. What I am saying is that I should have stayed. I should have allowed the Lord to vindicate me and correct my pastor. I was sore to my soul when I left. When I left, I was furious, which means that I rushed to get married. It was not because I was ready. I rushed to get married, not only from fear of fornication, but I rushed to get married out of anger for the way I was treated. I should have let the Lord heal my heart, but I didn't. I ran to an irresponsible and unequipped little boy, and expected him to do something that only God could do.

I needed healing.
I needed time.

Maybe I would have left my cousin's home and gotten my own home, eventually. The timing would have been right. I left my assigned home to mature, grow, learn, and submit. I don't know what I would have gleaned from my cousins when I watched them interact with their children and each other. My cousin had so much to offer me. She had so much wisdom. At that time, I went to her for a lot of advice.

However, I realized that she never asked me to stay. She may have felt like I would not have listened to her because I was so hurt and offended. Up until that point, I did everything they both required of me. I never showed any signs of disobedience. I wanted to be a part of them and their ministry. If I did not, I would have never uprooted the life I started to make in North Carolina. I was comfortable there, but I knew there was more in life, and I desired to do ministry the best way I could.

I was sure that I was headed in the right direction. Wherever you go in the world, you have to deal with the issues of your heart. I feared that when people, specifically men, would try to control or rule over me. Being in my cousin's home allowed me to deal with some of the same traumas I faced with my father. The strictness, the control, the excessive discipline, and the obedience needed in order to please Daddy were what I experienced. Here I was, a 26-year-old woman, yet I felt like I was being treated like their child.

We all had to listen and abide by whatever my pastor said to do. So much so that, even when my daughter was sick with a fever, he expected me to help out at a Toys 4 Tots event that he coordinated. So, the next day I helped out. However, my daughter was still not well. He definitely showed his disappointment with that. He said out loud that anyone in his house was going to work. However, I never disrespected him or spoke out of turn. I said all that to say, my obedience wasn't the issue. It was me not wanting to give up the only thing I owned...

My will.

I needed to sit down and be cultivated. I was the one responsible for my daughter. I was responsible for the clothes on our backs. I was even responsible for providing for myself and my daughter. I was as independent as I knew how to be, but I was in a place where my will was being stripped down. That was the very thing I fought to maintain because I had come so far. It was a painful reality to know that if I had taken more time to pray and hear from God, things would have gone differently. Unfortunately, I acted out of my emotions and caused myself much pain.

I realized that if I couldn't submit under the leadership of my pastor, even after being offended, then I wasn't ready to be anybody's wife. As a wife, I needed to submit to my own husband. I was used to running or changing my scenario if it was something that made me uncomfortable. I had to learn to stay in the fire until God instructed me to move. I often left jobs I had for similar reasons. I was exhausted.

Running from state to state was not the way I wanted to live my life. I was looking for the perfect man to complete my imperfect life, and I thought that was the definition of *WHOLENESS*. Not only was I unprepared for marriage, but I was also unprepared for leadership. *How could I lead anyone when I wouldn't sit still? How could I lead anyone when I didn't like to be offended, challenged, provoked, or uncomfortable?*

These were the dealings of the enemy to tempt me to abandon my identity in Christ. I had the heart to work everywhere I would go, but I did not have the discipline. I was extremely strong-willed and stubborn, although I considered myself to be a positive and kindhearted person. There was a dark side that I did not want to deal with, and the wrong people had a way of pulling it out. God was trying to show me what was inside of me now, so it wouldn't affect my future. Instead of fighting the enemy, I fought the people I loved. I would not stay seated long enough to receive my blessing in the midst of the adversity. I thought that meant my blessing was in another place.

Oh, how wrong I was.

CHAPTER FOURTEEN: THE ELDER & THE PASTOR

Throughout the years, and the various relationships I've had, all of which are not all mentioned, there was a clear picture that I didn't like to be alone. Regardless of having a father or not in my home, I dated a lot. I did not understand what I even wanted. I just knew my relationship with my father wasn't always pleasant. Some people always say that you go out into the world and look for someone who can love you like your father. They say you look for the same attributes that your father had. The truth of the matter was, I did not look at all. These men always approached me.

In all my years, I may have approached or pursued two men total. I believe a man should pursue a woman. You can call me old-fashioned when it comes to that. Unfortunately, the enemy, meaning the devil, sees exactly what you're going through. He knows and studies your fears. He studies your every move. He brings the type of people into your life that will harm and ultimately destroy you. All you have to have is a vacancy in your life. Satan will come in an attempt to destroy you and stop you from reaching your potential in Christ, especially in your youth.

I had many open wounds. I had many open doors. I might as well have invited the devil in myself, knowingly. However, I did not understand that a broken relationship with your father produced many broken relationships in your life. I honestly thought that if I just kept moving on, Mr. Right would walk into my life...eventually.

The saying is, *"The best way to get over a man is to move on to another one."*

I didn't believe in dwelling too long over one person when there were so many more out there. I thought that if I gave someone else a chance, who was better or could do better, I was winning. It meant that I was moving on with my life. I wasn't looking for anyone. I didn't even have a type. If anything, I was trying to avoid my father's attributes in men. I didn't look for sex-crazed or lust-driven men. I didn't want an alcoholic. I didn't want some man who was conflicted and hard to understand. I damn sure didn't want a strict man, and one who refused to show me any kind of emotion besides anger. I also did not want to feel any type of rejection! Yet, I walked around, sticking out like a sore thumb to the enemy.

So, at the first signs of trouble in a relationship, I expected the man to throw me away. However, because I was dealing with the spirit of hurt and rejection, I ran most times before the relationship ended and started a new one. I appeared to be cold and heartless, but the initial encounter with me was pleasant. I described myself as strong-willed, stubborn, and spicy. The men I dated were attracted to my independent soul. I acted as if I didn't need or want a man. That caused them to desire me all the more. I showed them that whatever they had to give me, another man could do the same, maybe even better. However, that side only came out when they tried to control me. Any signs of my father, I ran fast. It was a complete turn-off, which was why I didn't understand why I would want to date "my father," as the saying goes.

With all that being said, I was still a sweetheart and very compassionate. I wasn't clingy, but still passionate. I was far from perfect. I would bark at you really quickly if I felt attacked. Then, it would take a long time to bring me back down to earth. I just needed to know I wasn't being played. As I embarked on different relationships, they all had commonalities. In my opinion, the things that make men... "men," are generally the same. I did experience that only some things were different, but ultimately, they wanted the same things and acted the same. It was easy to detect things they would do that I would deal with. If it wasn't worth my time, I exited.

I expected Christian men to be different from Worldly men. However, my perception of my own father was already distorted. Because of my upbringing, I was confused about the love of my father, and the love of the father I couldn't see. *Was I really expected to believe that my Heavenly Father loved me more deeply than the one who bore me?*

My first experience of love was with my father. He was the first male figure who taught it to me. He set the standard of what to expect. He showed me what love should look like, which was contrary to the picture and lifestyle my mother gave me. It was all so confusing, but I learned to live with it. It was as if I were used to my father's bipolar personality. With each day, you never knew what you were going to get. As a child, that will affect you greatly.

My mother would always tell me that she feared what my future relationships with men would look like. She didn't want me to be with an abusive man. Although my father did not physically ever put his hands on my mother, she did endure emotional and a measure of verbal abuse. However, I did not see my parents fight or argue. My mother would either walk away or just go somewhere and pray about it. My father reserved that abuse to spew on his children. As his children, we endured emotional, verbal, and physical abuse. My dad was strict, and he didn't take any junk. So, talking back to him wasn't even taken into consideration.

As I got older, I needed an escape. I needed a way to get out all those emotions inside. I hadn't learned just yet how to share my troubles with the Lord. So, given the chance, whoever came at me, I was ready and loaded. I wasn't a troublemaker. I enjoyed my peace. However, there are evil people in the world who would seek to take that very peace just to make you miserable. I wished I had fought harder to maintain it. Instead, I let the devil win.

I got so tired of my black brothers, including the ones I lived with, disrespecting me. I did not understand that they were hurting too. They were only doing what they possibly learned from their parents. Sometimes, when I walked down the street, men would approach me. I would politely tell them I wasn't interested, and then I would get called out of my name. I became so used to the harshness that most times I assumed a man would speak to me in that manner. Therefore, when I was asked anything by them, I rolled my eyes and was quick with my tongue. I was here for it. Most times, they called me unapproachable or called me a bitch. Once I gave them a chance... if I did, the very next thing they came for was sex. They weren't interested in my mind or my heart. So, when I started dating, I did not cook, clean, or cater to a man at all. In my generation, we just looked to a man to do it all.

Looking at my mother, she did it all, including work. My father worked as well, but my mother kept the household. She kept us alive. Not just through prayer, but literally, all the love she gave caused each one of us to not have a nervous breakdown. Had it not been for her love and care, I'm pretty sure I would have killed all my brothers and my father in their sleep. I held grudges of some sort for them all. As you can see, I was well on my way to hating men.

I vowed never to be like my mother. I felt like women could never receive what they needed or wanted by being *passive*. I tried to live my life being the opposite, and this is no reflection on my mother. She is a dynamic woman, and the reason why I even have a relationship with the Lord. It was driven by her true love, which was untainted and pure, by far... the way a parent's love should be for their children.

However, it's just sometimes you are hit with the negative parent's attributes. As loving as I was, I wasn't going to let you hurt me so much. Then, I felt like I had a superpower that caused me to forget a person. That means when they hurt me, or if I hurt them first, I had the ability to forget that it ever happened by erasing them from my life. This explains why I continued to go from one man to the next. Some men, whether single or married, always wanted a chance with me because I really didn't have a "type," as mentioned earlier. I dated all kinds of people. I did not sleep with them all, but I gave them a chance to prove to me that they were worthy of my space and time.

  I wasn't God's gift to men. However, I was cute or whatever. I didn't think I was conceited at all. It was just that I had gone through so much already that I had a thing about people, specifically men, who would waste my time. Eventually, I started dating Christian men. I really didn't care for them at first. If they were anything like my father, living double lives, I wanted nothing to do with them. I just wanted the same person I saw in church every Sunday.

  That was not the case.

  I got the most freakiest, controlling, and arrogant church boys of all time. Besides a Sunday morning, I really saw no difference. They claimed to love Christ in front of people, but lived the same way as worldly men. In everything they did, they were carnal-minded. Clearly, I was no better. I was also a hypocrite. In most ways, I was following Christ, except in this area. I would always start out telling the guy that I desired a Godly relationship, and that I wanted us to go to church together. They would come with me... until they felt they had me. I wanted to keep them, so eventually, I compromised and gave in to sin. When I saw that it was affecting my relationship with the Lord, I would beg them to stop.

  Unfortunately, they told me it was too late and that I never should have started. They said to stop having sex meant that I didn't really love them. I say the word "them" because it was a term I often heard from Christian men. Then, they talked about how they wanted to marry me and so forth. I heard lie after lie. I was convicted because of the Holy Spirit living on the inside of me. What would happen was that I would ghost them. In order to leave the relationship, I would break up for minor reasons. I did not possess the courage to stand for Jesus, so I settled for anything.

  I was losing myself. I still didn't know what I was looking for. I was relieved to just walk away and feel peace for some time. Yet, in months to come, I found myself back in the same position. Only this time it was a new face, but this new one was more convincing than the previous.

Dating Christian men meant that I didn't have to *make* them come to church, and that we were of the same faith. However, we would still be unequally yoked. I was forming **"SOUL TIES"** that would take years to break. The residues of each man followed me like a starving puppy trying to feed off of its mother, but couldn't get a hold of her nipple. They continued on until they were fed.

I could not get free.

I liked the men I dated... in their faces, but I secretly hated them on the inside.

At that point in my life, I secretly hated myself for allowing anyone to define who I was. I was allowing the enemy to tell me who I was and how far I was going to go. I let the culture of society dictate what a couple should be and what a couple should do together. I did not let the Holy Spirit teach me. I refused to live according to the bible, even though I knew better.

So... why even be a Christian?

Christians follow Christ.

Nothing I did pointed towards his direction. I was depending on love from some man to dictate the love I was yearning for and lacked in my own home. The affection I never received was from the man I wanted to receive it from... **my father.** I wanted validation from an outside source, indirectly. My ex-boyfriend once told me that I wanted a man to "*rescue*" me. He was right in some ways. I didn't want a man for what he had financially, although a man should be a provider if what he desires is a wife. He should be able to take care of the family. However, what I was looking for far exceeded material wealth. The man I needed would need to see my heart and soul. Then, he would need to minister to those broken places. I needed a man who understood the real love of God. I needed a man who understood the love that Christ Jesus showed for his bride, the church, and how he gave his life for her.

That was my heart's cry.

Now, to articulate that need to a man was impossible. The Christian men always seemed to want what Christ demanded of them, but continued to struggle in the flesh. The lust of the eyes and the pride of life seemed to have captured them all. They all desired things they did not have. For some reason, money and sex seemed to be their answer to everything. I was just there to satisfy that craving.

I've dated ministers, elders, and a pastor, and I have come up with the conclusion that a man is only a man. If that man will not live a life that has been submitted unto God, then there is nothing that separates him from being ordinary. The Holy Spirit dwelling on the inside of them is what makes all the difference. Men are only Godly when they follow the principles of God and obey. If a man doesn't follow God, then he is not Godly or a Christian. His character should demonstrate Christianity. He has to bear the fruit of walking with the Lord.

This rule is for both males and females.

I was involved with men who were not submitted to God, but ultimately had a calling to do the work. They accepted the call, but did not maintain a life of surrender and submission to their leaders unto the Lord who called them. They gave in to their lustful desires. I expected the men in my life, who called themselves *saved*, to lead me into righteous living. I never expected to go backwards in my faith because of the sin we committed together.

I am not blameless in any of this. I gave my heart to these men. However, I was yearning for a difference, which was why I agreed to even date them. Surely, I felt that they would not have the same desires as a worldly man. In my experiences, that was the furthest from the truth. They were weak in their faith, which was one reason why they couldn't help me.

In the beginning, I would be excited to know that, out of all the pain and heartache in my life that I had endured, God attached me with a Christian man whom I could finally honor him with. I felt that I no longer had to compromise my relationship with the Lord now. Yes, it is true that I had my own issues. Yes, it is true that I probably needed to work out the underlying issues of my own heart. Maybe I needed to be alone in order to heal from the years of abuse in some ways. I did not pursue these men. I only decided to entertain these men for a while because of all the promises they gave. Any woman would have jumped at the chance to make their life better. *Who doesn't want to be loved?*

Beware of a quick fix.

Some things take time.

I still had not learned that it would take time to see someone's character and the fruit they produced. There was no way I was going to see that in a couple of weeks. However, sometimes when you witness a minister's, elder's, or pastor's life, it is pretty public. You don't get to see their private life. You only see what they preach. So at times, it's glamorized, and it looks powerful, holy, and uplifting.

You normally feel good around ministers of the gospel, and you should. They have a responsibility to teach and encourage the saints. So, it's normal for them to have this zeal and passion for the gospel. It's also normal for you to feel drawn to them for that purpose.

What do you do when approached for "other" purposes?

Women tend to feel like they are the chosen ones and are special. Out of everyone in the congregation, they feast their eyes on you, and then they take the time to pursue you. I started to feel like maybe that was the reason I had gone through so much hell in my life. It was because I was attached to something greater than I. Yes, that part is true, but that greatness should be connected to Christ and what he has done for us all, and not this one man. You don't glorify the Father in heaven by giving yourself over to a man. You glorify him by giving Christ your entire life.

I had this whole thing backward. With every relationship, I was stripping my virtue away. I was poisoning my witness inside of me. I was selling my soul, all because I would not take the time to deal with my own issues. I should never have expected any man to erase the trauma I faced. That was a job that only God could handle. He was the only one who could heal me and restore all the time I had wasted looking for love in all the wrong places. My vision needed to be repaired. My perception of what would make me happy was all wrong. There was a lot of growing I needed to do. I needed to relearn what "The Love Of My Father" really meant.

Months had passed after I left my church, and I wasn't healed. However, I pushed my way through every day. I still had to work and provide for my family. I continued to seek the Lord for strength and healing. I was still dancing with another ministry because it felt good to release some things in that way. I knew my life wasn't over. I just needed to get over the shame and betrayal. Although I had no reason to be ashamed, the fact that everyone knew my business bothered me immensely. I was also struggling with the fact that I didn't stay and deal with it. Most of the rumors were twisted and hearsay. Not many people asked me the real tea to my face. Sadly, people like to gossip and listen to lies. I had to trust that God would vindicate me and my daughter. I'm sure he did just that in ways that I will never know, but he does it in a way of his righteous judgment. I had to let it go and move on.

There was a particular elder who helped show me love and support through it all. I began to spend time with him, and we talked all the time. I always thought he was handsome. Plus, he smelled so divine. It was almost intoxicating. He would walk past me with his suits on, and I would have to do a double-take because of how he cleaned up. Nice clothes, nice shoes, but the way he smelled... that alone knocked me off my feet. He smelled of bergamot, leather, vanilla, tobacco, and sweet whiskey. Anybody who knows about men's cologne knows that having any of these spices within it is a recipe for disaster. You can literally eat the skin off of someone. I can't imagine how many times I fantasized about doing that.

When we would do something in church called the Passing of the Peace, a part of the service where everyone embraces one another and shares kind words, there were times we embraced. However, I could barely keep my focus on God. I know it's extreme, but a good-smelling cologne on a well-dressed, attractive man was my cup of tea. Of course, I didn't want to be attracted to a married man. I mean, I never saw him with anyone. He told me later that he was in the process of getting a divorce. I was okay with it because he lived in a separate apartment, and their marriage was *really over*. It had nothing to do with me.

From a legal perspective, it would not be deemed as cheating, but morally, it was wrong. I understood how it was to live separately from my spouse, especially when the intentions are not to reconcile. So, I dated who I wanted as well while the divorce was pending. At first, we were only friends. We would go out to eat, and I would go hang out at his place. He even had me around his mother. That definitely caused me to feel more comfortable and settled. At that point, we weren't talking about being together because we were only *hanging out*.

It was nice.
It was fun.
Not fun like amusement park fun.
It was cool.
I could let down my guard and trust him. I never felt like I owed him anything. He had just gotten out of a broken marriage, and he did not want to jump back into anything. Any day, his divorce would be final, and all he had to take care of was his children, but I was

not trying to be anyone's stepmother. It was like we fell into a *situationship*.

There was no title.

We did not define who we were together.

No one knew on my end.

We just enjoyed each other better that way. When he picked me up, he parked a few houses down, or we would meet up somewhere. We were hanging out at a hotel one day because he asked me to meet him there. He was doing business in the area, so it was common for him to have hotel stays. As we were watching television and talking, the moment became awkward. I felt myself getting silly, and he became a little more straightforward.

We were on the couch when he reached over to kiss me. He grabbed my face and just did it. Our kissing became heavier and heavier. I stopped and asked him what we were doing. I don't recall him answering me. I told him that I needed to leave because the hour was getting late. He asked me to lie in the bedroom with him, which was directly in front of the living area. He assured me that he was not trying to sleep with me. He just wanted to cuddle with me. I believed him. So, I followed suit. We just talked beside one another while lying on the bed.

Then, we started kissing again. He wanted me to feel him, which I did. However, I was reluctant and reminded him that he said he was not trying to have sex with me. Again, he told me that he wasn't, and that he just wanted me to feel it. He had on sweatpants, so access was very easy. My thoughts were all over the place. I was nervous and horny at the same time, but I knew I was not ready for whatever he was offering. So, I pulled back.

As I pulled back, he quickly pulled it out and placed it on his stomach. *Yeah*, that's exactly what happened. Now, at this point, my eyes caught a glance of it, which caused me to do a double-take.

Oh my goodness, were my thoughts.

He grabbed my hand and placed it on it. I touched it, and then I pulled my hand back. I was impressed. It was very nice. I thought it was a little ***too*** nice. Then, he told me that was all he wanted me to see. I kissed him one last time, he walked me to my car, and I left. We did not have sex, and I was happy about that. Unfortunately, when I drove away, I could not get the vision out of my head of how it would be for that *thing* to be inside of me. All I knew was that I was in a heap of trouble.

We dated for a while before becoming intimate. For Valentine's Day, he planned this romantic dinner in the same hotel we were staying. When we were done, we went upstairs to the room. He opened the door to candles burning all over. The bedroom had rose petals on the bed and the floor. I walked into the bathroom, and the tub was full of water with roses inside the bubbles. The floor was full of rose petals and candles. This was the first time a man had done something this romantic for me. Everything was so beautiful. For two people who weren't in a committed relationship, he sure was putting it on me heavily. I definitely felt special. I felt loved and appreciated. Every time he touched me, it was so sweet. He was very gentle with me, which shocked me because of his profession. I expected him to be more aggressive. I was glad that he had a perfect balance.

Yet, he was a man who was set in his ways. There wasn't much room for compromise with him. I normally went with whatever he wanted to do. When I did voice my opinion, I could tell it made him pull back. He was not used to it, or just didn't like women being combative with him. He was very strong-minded when it came to his opinions. Because he did things for me, I could tell that he didn't really need or want any advice from me. When we got into debates, which would be healthy at first, his goal was to always change my mind. He did not seek for me to understand. Instead, it was more about getting his point across. Being right was his posture. He wasn't interested in my views at all. At first, I could deal with his arrogance, but because of the kind of person I am, I knew it wouldn't last long.

To continue with our one and only Valentine's Day, it was special. When my bath was over, I met him in the room and we spent our first night together. I loved every minute of it. I looked forward to spending more time with him. He was a little older than I was... maybe by like five or six years. Some men act really immature when they are close to you in age. However, he seemed to be mature and very responsible. Most times when I went to meet him for dinner or other places, he would take me to the gas station to fill up my tank. I remember the first time he did that. He followed me to the gas station and told me to put my money away. I already asked the gas man for $20 worth, so he ended up telling the guy to fill it up. He told me that that was the least he could do since I came out to see him.

He knew exactly how to put a smile on my face. The gesture alone caused me to melt. I love a manly man, especially those who know what to do without you giving them a roadmap all the time.

However, this can backfire. He can have too much control, and you can lose yourself in what his "standards" are for you.

We enjoyed each other for the most part. We were both stubborn, so we had disagreements and did not come to a mutual understanding. At times, we just stepped back from each other until we missed each other, and one of us reached out. It would take a week or two for us to come back around. When we did reconnect, we acted like wild rabbits. We could not keep our hands off each other. He was very mysterious to me. He told me about a set of skills he acquired pertaining to his job. I knew of some of the things he did, but his other sources of income were a secret. I just knew he traveled quite a bit.

April came, and it was time to celebrate my birthday. He took me to Las Vegas for four days. I had never been to Vegas, so I was so excited. We stayed in this high-class hotel. It was so beautiful. Everything was inside this hotel. It had a mall, a pond that led outside, a club, and many restaurants. I was in pure bliss. I walked into the hotel room, and it was filled with birthday balloons and chocolate.

The only thing different in this relationship was that it was all ours. There were no Facebook or Instagram posts of how special I was being treated. Neither one of us told anyone, and for the sake of the church I attended, it probably wouldn't have been favorable for either one of us. He was my best-kept secret.

Although he knew my family and my mother loved him, we just didn't want to share our relationship until after his divorce. It was better this way in order not to expect or place demands on one another. I enjoyed our privacy. The fact that it was only temporary made us both discreet. We didn't decide on this. It kind of just happened that way. I think we both knew we just wanted to have fun. When people are dating, they jump into a serious commitment when they are not ready, so many times. I was good at doing that, but I did not want to ruin our friendship by jumping in headfirst. So, we kept our business to ourselves.

About the second day in Vegas, we went to see Boyz II Men sing in concert. It was so amazing. I was closer than I expected. Then, we had a wonderful dinner. On the third day, we went to the wax museum. That was also great. Something happened between that time, because we stopped talking. We actually had a fight. I only remember us getting into an argument, and he called me a bitch. I could not believe he said that to me. I went all the way off. I picked up a wine glass and broke it over his head. He was ok because he only had a scratch. He grabbed the glass from my hands, but the glass ended up stuck in my hands. Finally, he forced me to let it go. We were in the bathroom while he was cleaning up his blood, and I was cleaning my hands that were full of blood. That's when he called me crazy, and I called him an asshole. He left me in the room by myself for most of the day. I went walking around within the hotel, but I didn't know where he had gone.

Later that night, he came in. I could tell he had been drinking. Neither one of us said anything to the other. He got into bed and went to sleep. When he woke up, he went downstairs and brought us some coffee. He placed my cup next to me, and I thanked him. That was the start of us talking about what happened the day before. He called me crazy again, and I laughed. He made love to me several times that day. The next day, we flew back home. That was day number five. Out of all the pictures I took, I did not take one picture of him. We didn't take any pictures together. That was not only strange... but sad.

A vacation I will never forget!

We never had a fight and disrespected each other like that again. As time went on, we grew apart. Our lives did not connect besides our intimacy. Intimacy is not enough to continue with anything, much less a long-lasting relationship. I kind of knew what to expect. He moved from the apartment he had into a nice townhouse. It was about 45 minutes from where I stayed. I absolutely hated that journey. I would go late some nights and wake up very early to head back home to get ready for work. That routine got old real quick. I began to see him less and less at church, and then... not at all.

I saw him preach at other places. It was powerful, and all the more attractive. It had been some time since I last saw him, but when we connected again, it was romantic. I went to visit the elder out of the blue when he called, of course. I came over and he had laid down a thick comforter on the living room floor, lit some candles, and depending on the hour, had a nice dinner ready for me. One thing we loved to share together was Häagen-Dazs ice cream. As we attempted to watch a movie, we cuddled until the movie didn't matter any longer. The light from the television dimmed until it was no longer there. The only thing seen was two silhouettes in the dark. It was damn near perfect. Months passed, and we just didn't reach out. I guess we both realized that we were not what we needed.

No conversation.

No explanation.

It was just over.

I dated one pastor a few years before I dated the elder. I'm sure they knew one another, but were not friends. I wasn't into this pastor at all. However, before it all ended, I was in love with him. It started one day when we passed one another in church. There was a cookout happening on a Saturday afternoon, and there happened to be a few church leaders congregating in the front. I needed to go inside the church to use the restroom before I joined everyone else outside in the back. So naturally, walking past a group of people, you speak.

When this particular pastor addressed me, it sounded a little too sensual. As I walked inside the church and went to the bathroom, I felt strange. I was almost captivated. It had nothing to do with the way this man looked... although he was handsome. It had everything to do with what he said and the spirit behind it. I told myself that if I felt anything else when I walked past him the second time, it would satisfy my suspicion. I left the church, and this time, it was only him and one more person standing there. He asked me how I was feeling, and he addressed me by my name. I was shocked and began to blush. I told him I was fine.

He replied, "I know you are, but I asked you how you were doing."

This slickster was trying to trip me up. This cat daddy of a man was really trying to sweet-talk me. It made me laugh out loud. I proceeded to walk to the back of the church, where the fun was. However, I took a look back, and he gave me a wink.

My suspicion was accurate.

This man likes me, I thought to myself, but I knew he was married. So, not only is he not available, but I was also confused. I mean, this man could preach the roof off the house. He was charismatic, friendly, and he seemed to love people. However, I did not know him on a personal level. I only knew his name. I respected him all the more. I just didn't understand what he wanted with me. What I do know is that he did greet me the first time, and he said something nice to me the second time. However, I promise there were spirits at work because I felt them. They were trying to seduce and entice me. They had already gotten my attention.

I started to wonder how long this man was going to stick around. He stuck around long enough to hand me his phone number. Because I was the dance leader at the church at the time, I believe that was his opening. He gave me his contact information the next time he crossed paths with me. I quickly put the number in my pocket. It would be days before I used it.

I regret ever dialing his number... I knew better.

However, I convinced myself that it was only for ministry, and given the opportunity, I would address what I was feeling concerning him and our encounter. I really did not want to exaggerate the situation or create one when it didn't exist. However, my feelings were spot on.

I wish I were wrong.

A few days passed, and I used his number. I announced myself to him as if he'd already forgotten. He was well aware of who I was. He knew that I was confused, and he did not begin to understand the nature of what I was even calling for. He began to tell me that he's always known who I was. He called me "the girl who dances." Apparently, he asked someone. I didn't know whether to be flattered or afraid because I had a potential stalker on my hands. He wanted to skip all the small talk over the phone and talk to me in person. At the time, I was visiting my sister, so I let her know that I would be back.

My sister, Rachel, instructed me to be careful. She did not trust the situation at all. I told her that it was innocent. As I walked out of the house and got into his truck, I looked up and saw my sister looking out her window to see who I was with. After all, I didn't tell her. He took me to talk at the park up the street. He smiled a lot, and that caused me to feel really nervous. I don't know how it happened, but the next thing I knew, this man grabbed my hand to hold it. He told me that he wanted to take me out.

There was no way I was this darn gullible. There was just no way. I told him I had to think about it. Before I got out of the car, he reached over and kissed me on my cheek. He said he had been waiting to do that for some time, but for some reason, I felt like I was being set up. The devil had me right where he wanted me.

I walked into my sister's house, and she asked me, "How in the world did that happen?"

"I don't know," I told her. All I knew was that we did not talk about dancing.

"Isn't he married, Angie?" My sister asked.

I responded, "Yes, but he said he just wants a friend, and they are not together in that way anymore."

"I don't think you should be talking to him. He seems sneaky. Like, he really came to pick you up just to 'talk' to you?"

"Yes, he said he needed to explain to me in person."

My sister responded, "I hope you're not falling for that. Ang, I don't want you to get hurt again."

I told her that I would be ok. I said, "Don't worry about me. I'm gonna see what he wants. I'm not gonna let it get far."

She walked away shaking her head. I was disappointed in myself for having to tell my sister I was in *something*, before it became *something*. That conversation bothered me for the remainder of that day. I decided that next time Pastor called me, I would dismiss any ideas of being friends with me. After all, when you're married, there shouldn't be a necessity to have a friend of the opposite sex anyway.

What did he need me for?

I was not willing to find out. My sister was right. I had been hurt far too many times. The last thing I wanted was to stir up confusion and division in the church I attended.

A day or two later, he and I had that conversation. He said that he understood. He let me know that he wasn't trying to be disrespectful. He was just lonely and had always admired me. According to him, he had no intentions of reconciling with his wife, and they were no longer sexually active. He literally shared that his nights consisted of watching porn on the computer to satisfy himself. I tried to explain that maybe the porn was coming between them.

How can anyone expect to save a marriage when they are addicted to watching porn?. That's adultery in itself.

Some spouses expect their mates to succumb to the things those people do in porn videos. Most times, it's not realistic. It's more of an aerobic sexual encounter if you ask me. Besides that, bringing the spirit of perversion into your home is crazy. You think your spouse is thinking of you when you're having intercourse, yet they have an image of that porn star they couldn't have. Then all of a sudden, you're no longer good enough for them. I told him, as a pastor, he was wrong to engage in those activities and should know better.

I think he was captivated because I voiced my full opinion to him. I wanted him to understand from a woman's perspective. He told me that he would rather jerk off to those videos instead of physically cheat on her. I let him know that he was already doing that. As the days went on, I played his wife's advocate, which eventually turned into months. We would just go out to eat at times, or he would visit me. When he would visit me, we never went into my bedroom, and sex was never involved. We stayed and talked in my living room. I remember there were times he even had to take family trips, and we still communicated for hours. He called me much more often than I would expect a married man to do. So, I asked him about being intimate with his wife. I let him know that I couldn't get mad at him for it, and I actually encouraged it at times. He swore that was not what he wanted anymore.

Eventually, he explained the separation to his kids. He told me that they were the main reason for him sticking around. A lot of times, I would reflect back on my mother and father's relationship. I wondered if these were the same excuses he gave to other women to gain their trust. Growing up, I never understood how a single woman wanted anything to do with a married man with children. It seemed as if my days of judging and not understanding relationships, much less my father, had found me out. I was becoming my father in a lot of ways. I was compromising who I was because I felt sorry for someone else's pain and supposed misery. While causing my own internal war, I was bringing great dishonor to my mother, to my God, and to myself.

Since when did I fall for bull crap like this?
Was the Pastor lying or telling me the truth?
Did it even matter?
How was any of that my business?... I wasn't supposed to fix their marriage.

This was way out of my league. I tried to encourage him more and more to consider his wife's feelings. The more I did that, the stronger he came on to me. I thought I had not crossed the line because I had not slept with him. However, that line was crossed long before, emotionally. He began to give me money to help me pay my bills and my rent. He kept telling me how much money was coming into the church, and how much money offerings were. Yes, he had a job as well, but the church did bless him. He started to share his money with me. Before it was said and done, he wanted to prepare to move out of his house. Then, he began to talk about marriage with me. I was his best-kept secret. Everything we did was in the comforts of my home. We even had Bible study together.

I saw firsthand what his lessons were going to be. I told him that as long as he lived with her, we couldn't go further. At times, he would get upset because I would tell him that God did not honor what we were doing. He disagreed. He said that he was miserable and could not continue sleeping in another bed in another room. He said he wouldn't watch porn as much if he were getting what he needed.

"I am a man," he said. "I am a man with needs!"

I only remember one time that he tried to have sex with me. However, neither one of us let it get that far. I was in the bathroom, and when I opened up the door, he was in the doorway butt ass naked. My eyes scanned his body because I couldn't believe what I was seeing. Yes, I had seen a naked man before, but not him. I asked him what he was doing.

"Do you like what you see?" he asked.

"Yes!"

He said he wanted me to see what I was getting. I took a towel, put it around his lower half, kissed him, and asked him to please go and put his clothes back on. Thank God he listened, because ten more minutes of looking at his nicely groomed body, I would have given in. Other than that, we never crossed the line with intercourse. However, a few months before, we were kissing heavily. For the first time, we were lying on my bed. I told him that I could not have sex, and he agreed that wasn't what he was doing. So, we held each other. The thing is that our conversations were inappropriate. He told me what he enjoyed sexually, and I told him the same. He showed me how he looked, and as I stared at him, I gave him what he wanted, with an open mouth... I just wanted to see, and he was definitely excited for me to see. I stopped, and we both agreed that we couldn't start something if we did not intend to finish.

Sin and lust are real. Whether you're a Christian or a pastor, you are not exempt. Sometimes, I think the temptation was the worst for us. I don't know how we stopped that day from going all the way. When you give in to sin, it won't stop until it completely consumes you. No matter who you are! Your body yearns more and more for what the flesh wants. Internally, I definitely felt the fight.

The pastor said he had tried counseling several times before, and it only worked for a short time. He said that his wife would go back to the same methods of doing or not doing things. I started to ask him about himself and how he was changing the situation. I noticed all he did was complain about what she was or wasn't doing.

"I would hate to be her," I said. "Can anything make you happy?"

He tried to explain to me that it wasn't like that. He told me a lot of things he disliked about her, and how she even wanted to have another baby. However, he wasn't trying to hear that because he had already told her he wanted a divorce. Then, he tried to convince me that I would make a wonderful first lady of the church.

I knew better. Look how we started out.

I began to have nightmares. I had no peace. This went on for weeks. I knew our relationship was the reason. I began to resist his advances towards me. God was talking to me through his word and through my dreams. He was giving me a chance to repent and end the relationship before he exposed us. We were in church one day for some type of service, and a visiting preacher called him out. They told him that he was in a dark place and that there was somewhere he visited daily at about 3 PM. They instructed him to stop going to that place.

Most times at 3 PM, he was either talking to me, leaving my place, or doing something that involved us. As that was being said to him, a minister in the church pulled me to the back to reveal to me what the lord was showing her that concerned me. She told me, "When God puts a man in your life, you wouldn't have to hide him. You do not need to be someone's secret. They would want you to be seen openly. Don't care about anything they are saying or doing for you because it doesn't matter if the only place it's done is in your home."

After church was over, I had a talk with him about what was said. His head was truly in the clouds because he did not think that woman of God who spoke to him was talking about me. When I shared with him what was said to me, he also didn't think he was keeping me a secret. He thought the right people knew. At the appointed time, we would reveal our relationship to everyone. He let me know that I was not a secret, but that the situation could and would hurt many people if it got out too soon. However, he assured me he was taking the necessary steps to move out and get the divorce.

Again, I knew better.

I told him that something was going to happen. I was paranoid. I had no peace. If that wasn't enough to stop us from seeing one another, another word came to me. My mother had a spiritual daughter who was thinking of me and needed to talk to me. So one day, the same week as I was getting ready to pick up my daughter from school, I called her. At first, the conversation was just an update on my life, then it went left. The Lord allowed her to see too much, in my opinion. She started asking me all kinds of questions. She asked me if I had a friend I was dealing with.

"Yes, I do have a friend."

She let me know that she saw that I cared for him deeply. She also saw that I loved him.

"Oh, this man is deeply in love with you, Angie."

"Yes, that's what he said."

"I understand, but I see you having no peace and not being able to rest."

I remained silent.

I froze.

Then, she said those magic words.

She said, "This man is married and wants to leave his wife to be with you. He can't do that. God isn't in it."

"I already told him that," I said... *which I had.*

She informed me again, "You need to walk away from him. Cut it off completely."

She understood the pain of it all, but did not understand how I let it get this far.

"I didn't know it would," I said.

However, I assured her that I would end it that day, and I did. I spoke with him that evening about what I was told. He tried to fight my decision. I even told him that he could not leave her. He was upset with me because he felt like I was fighting harder for him to keep his marriage than for us to be together. I told him that I needed God to bless us more than my desire to be with him. I told him not to call me anymore or try to pursue me.

He continued to call me, and he begged me to let him see me. I was sick. I cried for days, but I did not call. One day, my sister came over and I had to explain to her how I broke up with him, and she held me as I cried. He happened to feel me and call me, as my sister was comforting me. My sister answered the phone to speak with him. I remember hearing her tell him that he had to leave me alone. She told him she was afraid that something like this would happen, and I would end up hurting. He tried to explain to my sister that he wanted to be with me and never intended to hurt me. However, he told her that he would walk away. He told her to tell me that he would never stop loving me.

As time went on, he checked up on me less. He assured me that he wanted to be there to comfort me and to let me know that he was very sad. He vowed never to forget me, knew I was perfect for him, and that I would make him happy. I let him know that I would never change my mind. Also, I told him I wanted and needed him to try again with his marriage... and that was what he did.

About two months later, I saw him at a church convocation, which is when different churches under the same umbrella come together to celebrate. I saw him and his wife several times, because the event lasted about three days. Our eyes connected. There was definitely a silent spoken language there, and we both understood what it meant. It hurt my heart, but at the same time, I knew it was the right thing to do.

CHAPTER FIFTEEN: ACCOUNTABILITY

When I look back over the years of my life and I take the time to reflect on the decisions I have made, I realize that I had choices, and what I chose weren't always the right decisions. If I could do a lot of things over again, I most certainly would. Some people say that you should never live with regrets. They say that everything is a learning experience, and it's not a safe space to live in the past. You will never forget it, of course, but to live there is a whole other story. It is complete bondage. However, that doesn't mean you don't remember some of those choices that detoured your entire life.

God is faithful, and he is able to redeem the time back to you, if he so chooses, but that comes with total repentance. The longer you take, the longer you wait. I can't help but think and know that a lot of things I did would not have been done, and I would be further in my life as I would hope to be had I not done those things. Yes, in some situations, I really thought I was doing the right thing. The only problem was that I did not weigh those things out according to the word of God. Had I done that, some of my self-inflicted pain wouldn't have been. Even making good decisions didn't make them God's will for my life. Life is full of trials and tribulations, so that part is unavoidable.

Lessons that are learned have to be experienced. They help grow and develop your character. They are there to make you stronger. These lessons are not made for you to continue in a vicious cycle of dysfunction. They are presented to you so you can get to the next level of your life. You cannot continue to take the bait of Satan, then blame God because you failed. Most times, God shows you what is really inside of your own heart. He shows you the sin that lies within. Satan comes as the tempter. He wants you to fail. He enjoys it when "so-called" Christians take the bait and refuse to consult God, the Father, about the decisions we make. If we did, then God would be glorified in those decisions and situations. Then, we would be victorious.

We could move on and receive the reward that he has in store for us. However, I would cry to God after the bad choices were made, expect him to restore me, and then go back out and repeat the same sin. All I was doing was switching partners. I was trying to get rid of the person instead of the spirit that continued to connect itself to whomever I dealt with. Also, because I was not healed or delivered, I continued to build soul ties. Imagine a picture of walking around with every man I dealt with, tied to my hips... and I was collecting them like trophies.

There were times when deliverance came, but as time went on, and I became weary in well-doing, I most certainly fainted. When that happened, the enemy was back with more demons stronger than the first. This time around, it was harder to break free. I tried to live a life worthy of my calling. Many times, I was walking straight, but there are weaknesses and shortcomings that I have that the enemy tried to intensify and cause me to stumble again. There was an answer. There is an answer. I realize that I chose to satisfy my desire to be wanted, needed, and adored, more than I wanted to obey my Lord. At times, I would see the way of escape, but did not take it because I didn't think it benefited me. I did not see the rewards in following Christ. Because of this, I continued to waver and stay out of God's will. It brought me great pain and disappointment.

When you're walking in disobedience to God, you are making a decision to follow your own will, which is nothing more than a path of darkness and gloom. I had to repent, forgive the men in my life, and I had to forgive myself. When I put the mirror up to myself, I was unrecognizable. What I saw did not reflect what I would hope to be. I excelled in school, I was social and friendly, and I did what my parents required. However, I was still empty.

Once those things were acquired, I thought the next best thing was a solid relationship. The world deems that to be the order of success after all. The fact that I was moving forward gave me a false delusion of success. The world teaches you to grow up, go to school, work hard, and get a man. They don't give you a blueprint or guidelines for when the "plan" fails. Unfortunately, the church doesn't even prepare you for life. You are just taught to pray over everything.

Pray over trauma.
Pray over abuse.
Pray over mental illness.

Sermon after sermon, teaching you to do something they didn't have the will to do themselves. I was born into the church, so the things I witnessed confused me all the more. I did not see the things I was reading in the bible manifested. I began to minimize the very power of the Holy Ghost that lived inside of me. The things I went through in life made it hard for me to receive the love from a God that I could not see. I had to come to terms that I was angry with God. I couldn't blame myself for my failures, and I couldn't blame the men in my life, starting with my father. So, it only made sense to me that I would blame God.

That's exactly what I did.

So, everything in my life was a result of my bad decisions, alone?

No, I don't think so, but it was time for me to wake up and recognize that I couldn't continue to live in a state of dysfunction because of my past. I could no longer trust man and put my faith in the process of life. I needed an answer. That answer would set me free.

I needed to find Jesus.

I needed to experience his love and light.

I could no longer hold on to the God of my mother and father because this was a journey only I could walk.

I had to give up my own will.

Give up my own ideas of success.

I had to give up my pride and stubbornness.

I had to exchange a lot of who I was to receive Jesus.

I did not know if it was worth it. I did not understand if he was worth it. After all, he gave me this life. So, he was the reason for it all.

God, if you're real, just change me then.
Just change my circumstances.
God, if you are real, then just change my LIFE!

CHAPTER SIXTEEN: THE LOVE OF MY FATHER

My Father

My Father had a sound that I could not hear.
It was hollow and complicated; you could only fear.

As I struggled to hear with my two fractured ears,
the distance grew vacant throughout many a year.

Ask me how I knew he was ever near,
because of the fresh fragrance of pain in the atmosphere.

True love doesn't lie, how I wish it did.
I wish it whispered sweet little words of safety.
Snuggled up in a blanky.
Keeping me ever so warm.
Never to be cold.

Only to be respected.
Instead, I was rejected and neglected.

Did daddy's love for me grow?
Did he reap where he didn't sow?
Could he have invested when he didn't know?

Did daddy's love for me live?
Did his love know how to give?
Teach his daughter to breathe?
Even when she is being deceived?

By the hopes and the lies and the silence itself,
Followed by the screams of disappointment that he placed on himself.

Anger has a whole new tone when it's met with no answers.
Resentment and judgment became my father's features.
Daddy's little girl became Daddy's worst nightmare.
When I discovered he didn't love me unconditionally, it shattered me into a thousand pieces.

I have something to give you.
I will hurt them for not being you.

You will live over and over again vicariously through me
Now, I can fulfill all my daddy's dreams.
Letting him see the best in me.
How he'd taken the time to ruin me.
Snatch my destiny, I can barely see.

Trapped my heart in a field of thieves
Waiting to become, yet he stole the keys
PLEASE SET ME FREE!!

    I loved my father. He was my superhero. I don't know where these ideas come from... they just are. Stretching my neck, gazing at his big, old eyes, looking down at me. Looking for the smile of confirmation that came from his lips. Admiring his brown chocolate skin that looked like mine. My mother had lighter skin, so I did not see myself in her, but my father was my everything.

    "Daddy's home," my sister would look at me and say.

    As I ran to see him, I asked him, "How was your day?"

    I don't recall him ever answering me. He would just pick me up and press his full beard against my face. As I screamed out in pain, he laughed because he knew how much I hated that, but I endured it because I knew it brought him great joy. When he put me down, my brothers stood there waiting for their expressions of love or even acknowledgment of their existence to be shown. So, my father put out his arm and knelt down. He instructed us all to climb onto his muscles.

    As he stood up, he would swing us all and lift us up off our feet. Our legs would dangle in the air as if we were swinging from a tree. My father was stronger than all of his children put together! That was why he was my superhero. No one could defeat him, and they dared not try. I tried to get my father to gaze into my eyes the way he did that day when I was about three or four years old. There was such a sense of satisfaction that I received in my soul. I don't think I was too young to understand what love was.

    I felt it.

    I would always feel it from my mother. However, my father was totally different. He did not display emotions often. When he did, you'd better be sure it was because something great was happening.

I was too young to know what alcohol was, but I knew that when he left on a Friday evening, he came back early on a Saturday morning with a huge smile on his face. He was extra silly. My father was also extra touchy. He was even extra loud. That always made me laugh. My sister would eventually stay away from him when he was that way. I didn't understand why she wouldn't want to be around our father when, in fact, he was the most exciting person in that state.

"Come on," I would say to her. "Let's go sit on daddy's lap!"

As she pulled me back, she told me, "No, don't do that."

I yanked my arm from her hand and ran to greet my father. No one was keeping me away.

My sister looked like my father when she was younger. She was eight years older than I. My sister was the firstborn of five, with me being the youngest. My father would look at her in a way, too. It was in a different way that he looked at her. He looked at her as though he admired her beauty. As if he were shocked that he created such a child. She also did right by him. She did what was expected of her. Even things that made her uncomfortable, she still did because she loved him dearly.

She told me that one day, when he was drunk, he pulled her by her robe and sat her on his lap. As I mentioned before, that was not uncommon for me to do, as I was younger. It took on a whole other meaning when she did it. He kissed her as well, like he always had done. Because my dad was drunk, I don't know if he realized the severity of what was happening. However, something made him snap out of it because he pushed my sister off of him and instructed her never to sit on his lap again. That action caused my sister to look at him differently. She was confused and hurt. Not only that, but it made her uncomfortable around him when he was drunk. They never had a conversation about it. I know that his love for her kicked in before the devil perverted his true love for his daughter. I believe that's when my sister knew that demons were real. I, on the other hand, had no clue.

As the years progressed and his alcoholism intensified, he didn't go to rehab. He was a functioning father, husband, brother, friend, coworker, and an occasional evangelist. He was very giving to those everywhere. He even gave people money and food. However, when it came to giving his kids anything, he was very stingy. The older we became, the more it felt like he disliked us, especially me and my youngest brother. Yet, I continued to obey him. I feared that I would never receive the love I once had as a little girl. This man, I did not know. This man, I didn't even like. He cared about nothing more than being a disciplinarian.

Who am I to judge my father's true intentions towards me?
Could I really measure his love?

Maybe not. I just know that he couldn't give me what he did not have

Why didn't he have it?
Was it because he didn't have his father around growing up?
Was it because his mother didn't have time to give it to him?

That answer rests with him in his grave. My father wasn't the kind of man who answered anyone's questions, much less my questions. It took me 'til the end of his life just to see a tear come down his face.

I will never know why it was so hard for him to love me. I will never know why it felt like he hated me so much. I will never understand why I never made him happy, no matter how hard I tried. I feared this man up until the end. His death made me realize that even my father couldn't escape everything. He had to answer the door when death came knocking. This force he could not ignore, and he knew it.

There it was!

That look that I so longed for. The look that said, "Let me stay here with you." The look that said, "I'M SORRY FOR IT ALL!" The look that said, "I WILL NEVER SEE YOU AGAIN!". That look that I had been desperate my entire life to see again since I was four years old, I was now seeing it as he was dying. Everything he couldn't speak or communicate to me throughout my entire life was said with one look... and I forgave him! He forgave me. It was all wrapped up with the tears that ran down his face when the tubes were in his nostrils. He knew it was the end. I embraced his death like a proud daughter who could say that I experienced...

THE LOVE OF MY FATHER

So, the journey continues to find wholeness. It continues to find meaning. I continue to take responsibility for the things that I have allowed in my life. I press on to receive guidance from my heavenly father, in spite of the detrimental relationship with my father that started it all. This was only the beginning.

Shall I proceed to share with you what came next?...

To be continued...